How to Quickly Grow
and Identify Godly Fruit

How to Quickly Grow *and* Identify Godly Fruit

Spiritual Path to Christian Maturity and Marriage

d. Yvonne Shotwell

iUniverse, Inc.
Bloomington

How to Quickly Grow *and* Identify Godly Fruit
Spiritual Path to Christian Maturity and Marriage

Unless otherwise indicated, all Scripture quotations are taken from *Today's New International Version* of the Bible.

iUniverse books may be ordered through booksellers or by contacting:

iUniverse
1663 Liberty Drive
Bloomington, IN 47403
www.iuniverse.com
1-800-Authors (1-800-288-4677)

Because of the dynamic nature of the Internet, any web addresses or links contained in this book may have changed since publication and may no longer be valid. The views expressed in this work are solely those of the author and do not necessarily reflect the views of the publisher, and the publisher hereby disclaims any responsibility for them.

Any people depicted in stock imagery provided by Thinkstock are models, and such images are being used for illustrative purposes only.

Certain stock imagery © Thinkstock.

ISBN: 978-1-4502-9758-5 (sc)
ISBN: 978-1-4502-9760-8 (hc)
ISBN: 978-1-4502-9759-2 (e)

Printed in the United States of America

iUniverse rev. date: 05/19/2011

Dedication

To my future partner, spouse, and husband, one hand-picked by the LORD himself. He has the faith of Abraham. He is a faithful father like God. He has the delivering power of Moses. He meditates on the word like Joshua. He hears the voice of the LORD like Samuel. He is my Christian brother and provider like Boaz. He is a mighty warrior and worshipper like David. He is wise like Solomon. He has the endurance of Job. He speaks the truth of God's word like Isaiah. He has the commitment of Paul. Last, he has the compassion and love of Jesus and walks in the fruit of the Spirit. Okay, I will settle for the compassion and love of Jesus and walking in the fruit of the Spirit. In addition to my future partner, this book is dedicated to those in the Body of Christ who have a true desire to really know the Lord Jesus Christ. It is my desire that this book will direct you down that path whether you have recently had the born-again experience, are a seasoned believer or you are somewhere in the middle of these two. For it is God's desire for you to be intimate with him and fellowship with him daily as your friend and father.

Contents

Preface

Since I have been single all my life, I know truly the heart of the one we call single. Throughout the years I have struggled with my singleness. There have been times when I literally despised my position and it seemed as if when I looked around at others who were married, they also seconded that notion. You see those were my thoughts at the time. Then there have been times that I thanked God that I was single after I listened firsthand to the woes and problems of those who were married, yes, even Christians.

But I am grateful that God did not give up on me, but he used my past insecurities and misunderstandings to shape me into the vessel that I am today. Now, I am not one to brag, but as I look reflectively to where I was in my emotional health and where I am today, I can see a big difference. Today I am secure. I know who I am and I know my purpose. More importantly, I know my God.

My heart cries out for not only singles, but those who are widowed, married, separated and divorced because you are all people who experience hurt and pain. In addition, this book is not only for those mentioned above who are Christians, but to all individuals because God has created us all and loves us all with an unconditional love. All of us have probably at one time or another experienced a void or a vacuum inside of us. When I think about my past I had such a strong need for love and acceptance that when I was given a little taste of it, I would suck it up like a good vacuum picks up the dirt off the floor. All of us need admiration, encouragement, love, and acceptance. These are God created needs.

Thus, I give this book to you my dear ones and as you read the words on the pages, it is my desire that the very life of love, peace, and joy that I now experience would be imparted to you as if you are the vacuum and you are receiving it from the very heart of God himself. The most important thing is to monitor your progress over the next months as you read, meditate, and put action behind the keys in this book. I promise if you do that, you will begin an exciting journey and you will only look back to ask yourself, "Why didn't someone tell me about this earlier?" In any case, it is never too late. Get ready to rise up in joy, peace, love and purpose as you take each key and open doors that you didn't know existed!

Although I am not claiming to be an expert, my knowledge comes from communicating with married and divorced men and women, singles, wise observation, personal experience, research, and most importantly the word of God and my personal fellowship and relationship with HIM.

I feel that I am qualified to speak on this subject because I have always been single and have learned through experience and inner healing how to love by personally being taught by the Holy Spirit. The Holy Spirit has shown me what love is and now that I know that I am loved, I can love.

THE APPLE OF MY EYE

(Love letter from a father to his child)

You are the apple of my eye
You are more valuable than the moon and the stars
Don't ever be surprised
When I loose the bars
Before you were conceived in the womb of your mom
I looked down and smiled and allowed you to be born
For a purpose I created you
Structured your body like I wanted to
You will find me only when you seek me
In me you will find all you need
Stand up, Stand tall, look around, don't fall
Remember, I am your all in all

April 5, 2002
d. Yvonne Shotwell

Chapter 1
God's Way of Loving

Sometimes the heart sees what is invisible to the eye.
—H. Jackson Brown, Jr.

In the world in which we live people often identify themselves by physical appearance or what looks good to the eyes. This can be very deceptive because what you see is not always what you get. It is very shallow to base any relationship decisions solely on physical appearance. You can see that it is all too often the reality that people live with. When everything else measures up there is nothing wrong with an attractive physical body. But let's keep first things first.

According to the wisdom that you will find in the word of God, he does not want us to base a relationship decision on what appeals to the eyes. The body is only temporary, but the soul and spirit of a person is what really determines who they are. I am sure this is not the first time that you have heard this said, but many act as if it is some new and strange fact. You must dig deeper into the interior of the person. The scripture says in *I Samuel 16.7*, "But the Lord said to Samuel, 'Do not consider his appearance or his height, for I have rejected him.' The Lord does not look at the things human beings look at. People look at the outward appearance, but the Lord looks at the heart." True, it is not always easy. But most things that are beneficial in life aren't always so easy to handle. You should heed God's example and look at the heart, which holds the true character of the person.

If a man and a woman are attracted to one another, there will be outward chemistry. Both of them will like what they see in the natural and this is perfectly natural. You want to have a physical desire for the person that you are interested in. People are attracted by different physical characteristics. Nevertheless, you should get to know people based on their inner character-that which usually doesn't change over time. Please do not misunderstand what is being said. Physical attraction is perfectly natural. You want to feel good about your mate, or the person that you are courting or dating.

Nonetheless, you should get to know a person based upon character, which is the true self. Physical beauty will soon disappear while character has the ability to stand the test of time. Perhaps this is why so many men and women are still single because they are waiting on a fantasy, which probably will never happen. Don't misunderstand me in saying this because I know that God sometimes has a purpose that some persons who are still single may never know. That purpose requires them to wait much longer than the average person, even though they truly sense that they are obedient and mature. In the end it is all about his purpose and destiny-marriage or not. *Proverbs 31.30* says charm is deceptive, and beauty is fleeting......This lets us know that you would make a wiser decision by following after character than charm and beauty.

What exactly is character? Everyone has it; it will be portrayed as either positive or negative. Merriam-Webster's dictionary defines it as, "one of the attributes or features that make up and distinguish an individual." So everyone has it, but the individual can help shape whether it is positive or negative. How can you determine if a person's character is positive or negative? The fruit of the Spirit is the gauge to measure godly character. *But the fruit of the Spirit is love, joy, peace, patience, kindness, goodness, faithfulness, gentleness, and self control….* (Galatians 5.22).

You do not want to have God's plan delayed or denied for your life because of falling in love with someone whose character is lacking. Furthermore, you do not want to marry a person whose character is lacking. Marriage is for progression and prosperity, not for one to start down a path of digression. Perhaps many married people have missed God's plan for their lives because they followed after their emotions or other selfish desires. Did she really say that? Yes, she did! Some married couples have heard themselves and not God. This is quite obvious in the number of divorces today, even among Christians. As a result these individuals must be taught so that history does not repeat itself with these unhealthy relationship patterns.

Mercy and grace are extended to these individuals because making unwise decisions could happen to anyone. Here are what appear to be some common patterns for choosing wrongly: Christian married a non-Christian, Christian married someone who didn't fit the plan of God for their life, and couples who married at the wrong time; though perhaps in the future this could have been the right person at the right time. If a man and a woman are married, they should not just get a divorce and base it upon the reasons that I have just mentioned. Each couple must be responsible, learn and grow from personal choices.

Even if you have married the right person, because of humanity there will be challenges. You should thank God for his grace in spite of your selfishness and lack of knowledge. He can help if you are in a troubled marriage. Seek godly Christian counselors in your local church or those referred by the church. Marriage is not to be belittled because it is a sacred covenant from God, not merely a contract between two people who can break it anytime one is not happy. You should be made aware of this. Although I am not claiming to be an expert, my knowledge comes from communicating with married and divorced men and women, singles, wise observation, personal experience, research, and most importantly the word of God and a life of fellowship with him. *Plans fail for a lack of counsel, but with many advisors they succeed.* (Proverbs 15.22)

Then again, you as singles need to find out how to love God's way *before* marriage. Knowing how to develop godly fruit can help both single and married couples. I feel that I am qualified to speak on this subject because I have always been single and have learned through experience and inner healing how to love through the teaching of the Holy Spirit. The Holy Spirit has shown me what love is and now that I know that I am loved, I can love. Each day God is revealing more of his love to me that is defined in I Corinthians 13.4-8. "Love is patient, love is kind. It does not envy, it does not boast, it is not proud. It does not dishonor others, it is not self-seeking, it is not easily angered, it keeps no record of wrongs. Love does not delight in evil but rejoices with the truth. It always protects, always trusts, always hopes, always perseveres. Love never fails.

Nevertheless, I feel that because I have always been single I can be more sensitive to the needs of other singles. In the past, for two years, I established an interdenominational singles ministry which brought together singles from various denominational and non-denominational churches. God has put an anointing upon me to teach about experiencing intimacy and fellowship with the Holy Spirit and loving outwardly God's way with agape love, which is primarily what this book is about.

A person does not truly know how to love until he or she is born again and has God's Spirit in his or her heart. *And hope does not put us to shame, because God's love has been poured out into our hearts through the Holy Spirit, who has been given to us* (Romans 5.5). Unfortunately, many people try to find love or fill the void of Jesus in their lives by seeking many things. Things such as pleasure, money, fame, education, careers, materialism, sex, and pleasing people could be found on that list. The Bible would label these individuals as carnal or worldly-minded. They do not have the fruit of the Spirit working in their lives according to Galatians 5.22-23 which every growing Christian have begun to develop. The seed is there, fertilization just needs to begin. How can I say this? *2 Corinthians 5.17* says, "Therefore, if anyone is in Christ, the new creation has come: The old has gone, the new is here!" In the Old Testament in *Ezekiel 36.26* the same idea is mentioned. "I will give you a new heart and put a new spirit in you; I will remove from you your heart of stone and give you a heart of flesh." The seed is the new life of spiritual regeneration when the believer accepted Christ as savior, though manifested fruit shows that he is Lord. *But the fruit of the Spirit is love, joy, peace, patience, kindness, goodness, faithfulness, gentleness, and self control. Against such things there is no law.* (Galatians 5.22-23).

These individuals who are seeking things to satisfy the love hunger inside are immature and walking in the flesh rather than the spirit as it is referred to in *Romans 8*. Sadly, many times this is done unknowingly. How can one know what it is that is right to do if they have not been taught? *Romans 8* is a power-packed chapter and you should read it in its entirety. *Verse 9-11* reads, "You, however, are not controlled by the sinful nature but are in the Spirit, if indeed the Spirit of God lives within you. And if anyone does not have the Spirit of Christ, they do not belong to Christ. But if Christ is in you, then even though your body is subject to death because of sin, the Spirit gives life because of righteousness. And if the Spirit of him who raised Christ from the dead is living in you, he who raised Christ from the dead will also give life to your mortal bodies because of his Spirit who lives in you."

Now a question has to be asked here. Are these singles or individuals who are following after the carnal nature the same ones that want to be married or perhaps are already married? You must give your entire lives over to Christ so he can do a work in you to have you transformed into his image. *Since you live by the Spirit, let us keep in step with the Spirit* (Galatians 5.25). If you, as singles, do this you will not have to spend the beginning years of your marriage letting God get the excess "baggage" out of you, but instead enjoy more marital bliss.

Garbage should be put in its proper container, the trash can, not your body, which is the residence of the third part of the precious Trinity, the Holy Spirit. This illustration reminds me of a message my grandfather preached when he was alive titled, "It is time to take the garbage out of the church." I can't remember exactly, but either he demonstrated the message or I suggested afterward that he should have given the church audience a visual picture that showed the actions along with the word of God which would then make the message even more powerful. The demonstration was to have a waste basket put at the front of the church and people had to write down what *trash* they had in their lives and walk to the altar and put it in the garbage. I don't believe anyone would forget that message and many would receive deliverance and freedom.

The time to be transformed by the renewing of your minds is now as it is written in *Romans 12.1* which says, "Therefore, I urge you, brothers and sisters, in view of God's mercy, to offer your bodies as a living sacrifice, holy and pleasing to God-this is true worship. Do not conform to the pattern of this world, but be transformed by the renewing of your mind. Then you will be able to test and approve what God's will is-his good, pleasing and perfect will." Offering your bodies as living sacrifices will allow you quicker access to knowing God's perfect will for your lives, which he is so eager to reveal to your broken hearts and obedient spirits; though he will never force his will upon anyone.

There could be a time period in your lives when God calls you to a "season of singleness." That does not mean that you become isolated or unfriendly. This would be a time when you are not dating. The reason for this is so that you can have all of Christ's character perfected in you and you learn to hear the voice of God. You will be taught to accept Him as not only Savior, but also as Lord. I think knowing him as Lord is a missing ingredient in the lives of many Christians. It is like you are baking a cake, but forget to put in the main ingredient-the flower. Something just ain't right! Well, without Jesus as Lord, something just ain't right!

When making Jesus Lord you learn to experience God's joy, not happiness. Happiness is circumstantial, while joyfulness is a decision of submission to be content at all times. God's love, joy and peace are experienced when you submit to his Lordship. You should get so emerged in God that you even forget that you have a need for a mate. During this time you are experiencing being *single and with a purpose.* You are satisfied with your relationship with God, because you have put him first and foremost in your life. That does not mean that you will not have challenges of being alone or lonely. You are human so that is going to be a great possibility, but you learn to make adjustments to fulfill that void through other godly relationships. And after you do this, for most I believe God will surprise you with a mate, if that is your desire and it is God's timing. Notice that this mate will be given without the pressures of outside influences. You should let Jesus be your perfect lover. Jesus will teach you how to receive and give love the agape way. *Love is patient, love is kind. It does not envy, it does not boast, it is not proud. It does not dishonor others, it is not self-seeking, it is not easily angered, it keeps no records of wrong. Love does not delight in evil but rejoices with the truth. It always protects, always trusts, always hopes, always perseveres. Love never fails.* I Corinthians 13.4-8

God will give you the desires of your heart, but you must walk in his wisdom. According to the creator and sustainer of the universe, the wisest person that has ever lived was King Solomon who was

King David's son in the Bible. Listen to how he gained such wisdom in *I Kings 3.5-15.* "At Gibeon the LORD appeared to Solomon during the night in a dream, and God said, "Ask for whatever you want me to give you." Solomon answered, "You have shown great kindness to your servant, my father David, because he was faithful to you and righteous and upright in heart.

You have continued this great kindness to him and have given him a son to sit on his throne this very day. Now Lord my God, you have made your servant king in place of my father David. But I am only a little child and do not know how to carry out my duties. Your servant is here among the people you have chosen, a great people, too numerous to count or number. So give your servant a discerning heart to govern your people and to distinguish between right and wrong. For who is able to govern this great people of yours?"

The Lord was pleased that Solomon had asked for this. So God said to him," Since you have asked for this and not for long life or wealth for yourself, nor have asked for the death of your enemies, but for discernment in ministering justice, I will do what you have asked. I will give you a wise and discerning heart, so that there will never have been anyone like you, nor will there ever be. Moreover, I will give you what you have not asked-both wealth and honor-so that in your lifetime you will have no equal among kings. And if you walk in obedience to me and keep my decrees and commands as David your father did, I will give you a long life. Then Solomon awoke and realized it had been a dream."

Why am I talking about Solomon here? Solomon was one who knew enough to know that he could not make the best decisions without God's hand in his life. He was young and inexperienced. You need to have a wise and discerning heart like Solomon had before you say yes to marriage. You need to have inner wholeness and experience that personal relationship and fellowship with Christ so you truly know who you are and what kind of marriage partner would be suitable for you. In the ancient writings of Proverbs, Solomon gives lots of advice on wisdom and understanding.

Proverbs 1.7 says, "The fear of the LORD is the beginning of knowledge, but fools despise wisdom and instruction." *Proverbs 2.6* further states, "For the Lord gives wisdom, and from his mouth comes knowledge and understanding." *Trust in the Lord with all your heart and lean not on your own understanding; in all your ways submit to him, and he will make your paths straight.* (Proverbs 3.5-6) Last, but certainly not all, from these ancient writings in the Old Testament of the Bible, is "*Do not forsake wisdom, and she will protect you; love her, and she will watch over you. The beginning of wisdom is this: Get wisdom. Though it costs all you have, get understanding. Cherish her and she will exalt you; embrace her and she will honor you.* (Proverbs 4.6-8)."

Wisdom is the key to everything. Wisdom is really needed when seeking a marriage partner. Many people love to hear about the romantic kind of love between a man and woman. Yes, this is very natural. God made male and female for each other. In Genesis, I believe Adam would have been content without Eve if he needed to. Why do I say that? Well, he didn't know what he was missing, even though he was lonely. I believe God could have filled that void without Eve because even if you marry and you are not a whole person you will still feel like something is missing, and that something is the agape love from the Lord. Let us look in Genesis 2. The Lord God said, "*It is not good for the man to be alone. I will make a helper suitable for him.....So the Lord God caused the man to fall into a deep sleep* (Genesis 2.18, 21-24).

God was the one who decided that it was not good that the man should be alone. God was the matchmaker and neither had to pay a monthly fee. Some of you know what I am talking about with the internet dating popularity. All joking aside, God can and does use these services, if he so chooses, as a tool to bring two people together, but I think you understand my point.

Adam was unconscious; he was in a state of rest and relaxation. He was not aware that God was making and preparing a wife for him. While Adam was sleeping, God went inside of him. Within Adam's very heart and inner being, the master took a rib from this man's side and made Eve (Woman). The rib was Adam's support piece. Because both male and female were already inside *Adam* (*mankind*), Eve basically was just taken out to be the female Adam. They were already one. God presented the woman to the man (see also Proverbs 18:22). Eve did not go searching for Adam. Eve was now to be placed at his side or alongside Adam. This was a place she had already been so when she saw him she probably felt as comfortable as Adam did. She should have felt that she was going back to a place where she had already been. This is how it should be when singles find the one that is for them. It should give you an "I have already been here" feeling.

God for his own reasons had made the first *mankind* to take on the image of the *male* man instead of the *female* man. They had a connection in the flesh because they were already one from the beginning. Notice that I said flesh. I am not neglecting the spiritual connection. I am already assuming that because you are spirit, soul and body. There must be that spiritual connection first for Christians. Your mate should be a Christian too. Adam said that Eve was bone of his bones and flesh of his flesh because he recognized himself. Because of this, man was supposed to leave his father and mother and connect with his wife or reconnect with himself.

One problem that you have today is that couples are not leaving their mothers and fathers emotionally or financially, even though they might not be living with them in the same physical building. And I hope this goes without saying that your siblings or any other relatives should not be interfering with your marital relationship. When couples do not leave and cleave they can not totally connect with their mates. In order that this and other problems do not affect you as a single, you must get God's choice of a mate. Allow God to bring your spirits, souls, hearts, and purposes together so that you may flow with the Holy Spirit and God's plan for your life.

All of us want to be loved. That is how we were created in the image and likeness of God. God is love. But the problem is some of you are looking for love, but in all the wrong places, people and things. I believe there was a popular song called 'lookin for love in all the wrong places' many years ago. There was a lot of truth in that particular line of the song. Even the writer and perhaps the singer of that song knew that real love could only be found in certain places. You must first learn to love yourselves before you can even think about loving someone else. Some of you might already love yourselves too much and should give out the love that you already have. God tells us to love our neighbors as ourselves. You see this in Matthew. *And the second is like it: 'Love your neighbor as yourself* (Matthew 22.39).' But if you do not know how to love yourselves, then you will not be able to love your neighbors. This could be why there are so many people who can not get along with others. They are missing the fruit of the spirit of love. Love is not self-centeredness. If you are centered continually on yourself that does not necessarily mean that you love yourself. Love does not cause harm, so if you are causing harm to yourselves in any kind of way then that is not love, but sounds more like hate actually.

People choose often to love others, or perhaps I should say admire or be infatuated with people based upon: physical appearance, possessions, wealth, or what they can do for them. This is a mistake. Some often try to love by becoming involved in immoral, unholy and unhealthy relationships. A need for love is understandable, but often you do not know where or how to find it. Please do not misunderstand me. I am speaking of those singles or couples who have not totally committed themselves to Christ, given Him Lordship, and allowed the fruit of the Spirit to be active in their lives. God is a god of a second plus chance. So if you made some wrong choices he stands at the door of your heart to immediately forgive you and you should immediately receive that forgiveness and move on to purpose and destiny.

Sometimes this strong need for love can even go back to a lack of love during the childhood and teenage years. How can you give someone something that you do not have yourself? I keep stressing this fact because it is often the missing ingredient in relationships. How can a person share food with someone who needs it if they have none themselves? If two people are looking for love and neither one of them have it, then that spells disaster. You do not know how to love God's way until you believe in Jesus Christ and his Holy Spirit comes to live in you. Now, I have known some non-Christian couples who were able to survive in a marriage but they could have experienced love God's way if they had the indwelling of the Holy Spirit. This would take their relationship to a whole other level. Without God you can only go so far as is humanly possibly in the depth of your love.

You might be saying how do I get this love and the Holy Spirit? Well, it is a multi-package deal because you get the love of the Father, the Son, and the Holy Spirit. *And hope does not put us to shame, because God's love has been poured out into our hearts through the Holy Spirit, who has been given to us* (Romans 5:5). Even more is in *Romans 10.8-13*. But what does it say? "The word is near you; it is in your mouth and in your heart," that is, the message concerning faith that you proclaim: If you declare with your mouth, "Jesus is Lord," and believe in your heart that God raised him from the dead, you will be saved. For it is with your heart that you believe and are justified, and it is with your mouth that you profess your faith and are saved. As the scripture says, "Anyone who believes in him will never be put to shame." For there is no difference between Jew and Gentile-the same Lord is Lord of all and richly blesses all who call on him, for, "Everyone who calls on the name of the Lord will be saved."

Let us return back to love as it relates to loving outwardly. Look at what the scriptures tell us about loving our neighbor in *Matthew 22.37-39*. Jesus replied: "'Love the Lord your God with all your heart and with all your soul and with all your mind.' This is the first and greatest commandment. And the second is like it: 'Love your neighbor as yourself.'" God is telling us to love him with everything that is in us. It further states in verse 39 to love your neighbors as yourself. First, you must love God and then love your neighbors. You can not love your neighbors until you get the love that you need by loving God unreservedly. How is this? When you get God in your heart, soul and mind, he will permeate every area of your life, which also includes your neighbor.

If I asked everyone who reads this book the definition of love, I would probably get as many different definitions as there are people because we are individuals with various experiences and personalities. Each answer may not necessarily be wrong. If you notice the biblical definition of love, then you will realize that a lot of it is the fruit of the Spirit. Perhaps, if the fruit of the Spirit are developed in your life you will then know how to love. *Love is patient, love is kind. It does not envy, it does not boast, it is not proud. It does not dishonor others, it is not self-seeking, it is not easily angered; it keeps no record of wrongs. Love does not delight in evil but rejoices with the truth. It always protects, always trusts, always hopes, always perseveres. Love never fails. But where there are prophecies, they will cease; where there are tongues, they will be stilled; where there is knowledge, it will pass away* (I Corinthians 13.4-8).

You must love your mate according to God's definition of love; even at those times when you are angry, impatient and unkind. You can not envy one another. You must not keep record of things or situations that have happened in the past that were negative in nature. Forgiveness must take place. Revenge for one another must not be sought. If your neighbor (anyone who knows you) reads this and compared you with scripture in your actions of loving them, would they say that you are practicing love? Would they say that you love yourself, since you are supposed to love your neighbor as yourself? Let me take it a step further. Are you ready to love a man or woman this way? If your answer is no, perhaps it might be best if you wait on marriage until you can answer yes because it will make both of you much easier to live with.

Because of Christ's death on the cross and by us accepting him as our Savior, we are no longer under the law. We are free from sin. Jesus now lives within us, and we are becoming like his very nature and character. Notice that I said becoming which means that a person doesn't totally change automatically after they are born again. But I have known those whom God supernaturally went down into the depths of their beings and changed them instantly. But for most people change comes with time. You should depend on Christ and his love to help you as you live in the natural by faith. *I have been crucified with Christ and I no longer live, but Christ lives in me. The life I now live in the body, I live by faith in the son of God, who loved me and gave himself for me* (Galatians 2.20).

Christ's love is beyond natural understanding. But his love is available to you as you seek him to know him in all his fullness. *And to know this love that surpasses knowledge-that you may be filled to the measure of all the fullness of God* (Ephesians 3:19). Therefore, you should not let anything come between Christ and you. This would even apply to your desire for marriage.

A man or woman should not separate you from the love of Christ and living holy. It does not matter how they make you feel loved or how nice they are. In fact, any right relationship will bring you closer to God. *Who shall separate us from the love of Christ? Shall trouble or hardship or persecution or famine or nakedness or danger or sword? For I am convinced that neither death nor life, neither angels or demons, neither the present or the future, nor any powers, neither height* nor depth, nor anything else in all creation, will be able to separate us from the love of God that is in Christ Jesus our Lord* (Romans 8.35, 38-39).

Do you love Jesus? Jesus tells us how to love him. *Whoever has my commands and keeps them is the one who loves me. Anyone who loves me will be loved by my Father, and I too will love them and show myself to them* (John 14.21). Are you prepared, if circumstances called to give your life for another? True love is not self-focused, or focused inwardly, but other-centered or focused outwardly.

This is how we know what love is: Jesus Christ laid down his life for us. And we ought to lay down our lives for one another (I John 3.16). *Greater love has no one than this: to lay down one's life for one's friends* (John 15.13). There is no love that you can get that will equal or surpass the love Christ gave us when he died on the cross for mankind. Jesus gives us the best model for love. Love should be other-centered, not selfish. Not too many of us would be willing to die for another.

Relationship Analysis
When Love is Not Mutual-Jacob and Leah

Let us take a look in the word of God in *Genesis 29.15-30* at an interesting relationship of unrequited love. "Laban said to him, 'just because you are a relative of mine, should you work for me for nothing? Tell me what your wages should be?' Now Laban had two daughters; the name of the older was Leah, and the name of the younger was Rachel. Leah had weak eyes, but Rachel had a lovely figure and was beautiful.

Jacob was in love with Rachel and said, 'I'll work for you for seven years in return for your younger daughter Rachel.' Laban said, 'It's better that I give her to you than to some other man. Stay here with me.' So Jacob served seven years to get Rachel, but they seemed like only a few days to him because of his love for her. Then Jacob said to Laban, 'Give me my wife. My time is completed, and I want to make love to her.' So Laban brought together all the people of the place and gave a feast. But when evening came, he took his daughter Leah, and brought her to Jacob, and Jacob made love to her. And Laban gave his servant Zilpah to his daughter as her attendant. When morning came, there was Leah! So Jacob said to Laban, 'What is this you have done to me? I served you for Rachel, didn't I? Why have you deceived me? Laban replied, 'It is not our custom here to give the younger daughter in marriage before the older one. Finish this daughter's bridal week; then we will give you the younger one also, in return for another seven years of work.' And Jacob did so. He finished the week with Leah, and then Laban gave him his daughter Rachel to be his wife. Laban gave his servant Bilhah to his daughter Rachel as her attendant. Jacob made love to Rachel also, and his love for Rachel was greater than his love for Leah. And he worked for Laban another seven years."

Leah was the eldest of Laban's two daughters and based upon the customs of the time the oldest daughter should be married first, but Laban failed to discuss this with Jacob before they made the agreement for him to serve to get Rachel as his bride. He was deceived by Laban. Perhaps he was reaping what he had sowed because he deceived his father for the blessing. It should have gone to his older brother Esau, but instead he pretended to be his brother and because his father was old in years and was losing his sight he blessed Jacob instead (see Genesis 27).

But I really want to focus on Leah who was given to someone that did not love her. Can you imagine how excited she was about her future groom and their wedding day? She might have been thinking that it has finally happened. Is it really me getting married? Am I dreaming? Let me pinch myself. She was riding the clouds, only to be in the valley after one week of being *the one*. Of course back then she was still married to Jacob, but it was out of obligation and not love. I wonder how many marriages are like that today-just because of financial need, the children, or to present the correct image to society. You need to make sure you find out who you are marrying before you say "I do." You must not let the enemy deceive you, especially for a very important decision as finding a lifetime mate. I believe the most important decision one can make in his or her life is to accept Christ as Savior and Lord and after that the most important would be choosing the right person to marry. Why? Both of these decisions will determine your two futures-one in heaven and the other on earth. Jacob loved Rachel more than he did Leah. There was nothing Leah could have done about that because of the times they lived in. She had no voice in who she would marry. Or in some cases a very small voice, if any. But still, I would imagine Leah felt rejected, misused and alone; probably somewhat depressed and feeling like she was less of a person and woman. How many of you can empathize with that?

Again and again, God steps in to help heal and love those who are hurting. He is full of grace. He opened Leah's womb. A son was born. Because God had seen Leah's *misery*, he was named *Reuben*. Leah thought in her heart and mind that Jacob would love her. Why? Rachel was barren and could not give him what every man desired, a son. Well, now Leah had something to offer Jacob. How many women can identify with that feeling today? You got pregnant on purpose thinking that your man would marry you or if you were already married then perhaps you thought he would love you more and give you the time and attention you desired. But after the baby arrived he might have remained the same, left you for another, and/ or resented you for your tactic of seemingly trapping, manipulating, and controlling him and the situation. Be warned ladies it doesn't work. This is one of the oldest tricks of women and one of the most deceptive tactics of Satan to destroy your life. You will be stuck with a child, a confused and lonely life and in need of more finances to rear the child alone, or if you are married you will have less time to do things you enjoy for yourself. Neither situation got the woman what she really wanted-the love of the man. Many times women try to manipulate or even please others by doing things that are against their desire or moral standards just to be loved and accepted. Here's truth in case you are wondering. Taking things into your own hands usually don't help, but makes the situation even worse.

Later, another son was born and he was named Simeon. Then Levi was born. She knew that after this surely Jacob would love her and become attached to her. Leah might not have been the most loved or beautiful woman, but she did not have any problems birthing babies for sure. Her womb was blessed. Finally, she had her fourth son, which led her to *taking her eyes off her own selfishness of seeking love.* His name was *Judah.* Leah *praised and worshiped* the *Lord.* Leah began to realize these sons were for God's glory and purpose and not for her own glorification. I believe that the relationship between her and God was becoming more real and she was finding out she was special in God's eyes. Isn't that how it often works? When you have finally done it your way and see that it just isn't working, then you surrender to the Lordship of Jesus and receive the joy of the *Lord.* God stands there with open arms full of Grace to receive us.

Chapter 2
Are You in Need of Patience?

Patience is the companion of wisdom. Saint Augustine

Having the fruit of the Spirit of love is the foundation for all other fruit. Without love it might be difficult to grow the fruit of patience. Fruit is a product of life. If there is no fruit, then there is no life. There may be existence, but no life. Yes, it is true that Christians have the Spirit in them, but it is up to Christians to follow and keep up with the Spirit. When believers walk with the Spirit, they do not have their own agenda. They are seeking God's will and purpose for their lives. When single believers wait with patience on God he will bring their mate. *Since we live by the Spirit, let us keep in step with the Spirit* (Galatians 5.25).

Patience produces character and tests our motives. It also keeps us from making foolish, worldly decisions. Character is what develops us in all areas of our life. If you have hope, then you still have a chance for God to give you the desires of your heart. Our hope is the love of God that you have in your heart. You have God's power on the inside of you. *Not only so, but you also glory in our sufferings, because you know that suffering produces perseverance; perseverance, character; and character, hope. And hope does not put us to shame, because God's love has been poured out into our hearts through the Holy Spirit, who has been given to us* (Romans 5.3-5).

Anyone can easily hope for what they see. Can you hope for something that you do not even have the slightest sign that it is going to come to pass? You have to wait and have faith in God for your mate. You have to stand on God's word and promises. Faith and patience will be developed while you wait whether you want them to or not. *But if you hope for what you do not have, you wait for it patiently* (Rom 8.25). Patience also tests your faith. *Consider it pure joy, my brothers and sisters, whenever you face trials of many kinds, because you know that the testing of your faith produces perseverance. Let perseverance finish its work so that you may be mature and complete, not lacking anything* (James 1.2-4). But the good thing is that in the midst of the trial God changes our wrong desires to coincide with his purposeful desires and we come out of the test more mature and complete, and having all our needs met. Our wants would have changed also to be more in line with the father's will. When this happens you will find yourselves wanting less of what you thought you had to have. This transformation brings forth pure peace and joy.

Why would you count it joy when you are going through trials and tests? If you yield to the life-changing word and power of God he is going to transform you through his word into someone that you never even imagined possible. How is this? God's word says, *For my thoughts are not your thoughts, neither are your ways my ways, saith the* Lord. *For as the heavens are higher than the earth, so are my ways higher than your ways, and my thoughts than your thoughts* (Isaiah 55.8, 9).What does this scripture really mean? What will happen is that your mind will be changed. God will take you from worldly and carnal thinking to thinking like one who is righteous. Not only that but your actions will follow your thoughts and in this sense you will have truly become new creations in Christ.

This goes back to the fact that experience equals hope. The past gives us experiences that we should look at and study to learn from so that we will not repeat wrong decisions. And if you happen to forget and repeat one then you should learn from that and try not to repeat it a third time. Hope also comes through encouragement from the Word of God. You should not only look at your own experiences, but also those of other men and women of faith, as well as from those more mature Christians in your life. *For everything that was written in the past was written to teach us, so that through the endurance taught in the Scriptures and the encouragement they provide you might have hope* (Romans 15.4). My dear friend isn't that what the Bible is for? It is written to give us hope during those times when we feel like giving up on life and everything that is a part of us.

As you can see patience and hope are closely connected. The reason why some of us do not get results from God, or get God's choice of a mate is because we do not persevere. You hear the word, retain the word, but do not let the word have its *perfect* work. Therefore, instead of producing a bumper crop (God's mate), the seed remains and it never grows. What is a bumper crop some of you might be saying? Well, I have heard the term *bumper crop* many times when I was growing up, but researched it to get a better understanding and how it applies to waiting on God for a mate. It supposedly originated in the 1700s when the harvest was so large that it caused the containers or baskets used to ship things to market to swell.

What caused the harvest to be so great? The right conditions such as a good environment of sun, water, soil, and fertilizer that helped give the crops the right nutrition. How do you get a bumper mate from God? You must create the right conditions, which is what you are learning about in this book, primarily developing your character through the fruit of the Spirit. Wrong decisions are sometimes made to choose someone who is not good for you. At this point you find that you are not in God's good, pleasing, and perfect will according to Romans 12.1,2. If you choose someone who is not a Christian then you have a defective seed. Don't get me wrong. The person is not defective, but your partnership with them is defective because it is not God's perfect will.

Why did you choose a defective seed? This happened because you did not present your body as a living sacrifice to be used the way God wanted and in God's timing. Luke helps us with this thought. *But the seed on good soil stands for those with a noble and good heart, who hear the word, retain it, and by persevering produces a crop* (Luke 8.15). I am not saying that the non Christian is defective, but he or she is not the right match for a Christian because you have different beliefs and perspectives. It is impossible for the two to become as one in a spiritual sense. His or her seed does not have the Spirit of God in it, though they are God's creation and have a conscious to know how to determine right from wrong.

Now, the person is still human and might have a good heart, great job, and many other things. But the Bible tells us as Christians that you should not date or marry unbelievers. *2 Corinthians 6.14* tells us this, "Do not be yoked together with unbelievers. For what do righteousness and wickedness have in common? Or what fellowship can light have with darkness?" Because the Bible writers lived in a time where farming or agricultural science was the major source of providing a living, often the writers and Jesus himself would use illustrations that the audience of the time would understand.

When something is yoked it is harnessed usually with a type of wood to make the two become as one. Animals were yoked together primarily at the head or neck. I had this thought that if we as Christians get yoked together with someone then the two of us become one. That means that everything that they are we now become and vice versa. Can you see that picture? You can't tell what it is. The head is the guide so if you have two heads going in different directions you will either never get moving or one of you will be going somewhere that the other person doesn't want to go. As singles you must be careful to yoke up only with someone who loves God and has the fruit of the Spirit working in his or her life. Jesus gives us some good advice about being yoked. *Take my yoke upon you and learn from me, for I am gentle and humble in heart, and you will find rest for your souls* (Matthew 11.29). If you need to be yoked then God wants you to first of all be yoked with his love, his Spirit, and his word, which will allow you to daily rest in his peace and not be fretful.

You can do the will of God and still not receive the promise if you will not endure, persevere and wait patiently on God's plan. Hebrews 12.1-3 tells us to run with patience. *Therefore, since we are surrounded by such a great cloud of witnesses, let us throw off everything that hinders and the sin that so easily entangles. And let us run with perseverance the race marked out for us, fixing our eyes on Jesus, the pioneer and perfecter of faith. For the joy set before him he endured the cross, scorning its shame, and sat down at the right hand of the throne of God. Consider him who endured such opposition from sinners, so that you will not grow weary and lose heart.*

This is not a picture of a sprinter, but a distance runner which brings forth endurance. A sprinter brings on all his or her strength in the beginning and keeps the intensity or even somehow forces even greater intensity through the finish line. But remember sprinting is only good for short distances in which you can see the finish line or your final destination. In distance running you usually can not see the finish line with your natural eye until you are actually very near to it. In distance running you definitely do not need anything pulling against you or slowing you down. If you get off your pace, it is going to take double the strength to regain it again. I know this personally because during my teenage years I competed in track and field. If you happen to lose your pace, you should put your eyes back on the target, which is Jesus Christ. It is God who has begun and will end the race. Do not let your past mistakes or any person keep you from running *patiently* with God. Remember, if you are knocked down, there is still hope if you keep your eyes on Jesus.

Relationship Analysis
Creating An Ishmael-Your Choice, Not God's
Sarah/Abraham/Hagar

Love Triangle

N *ow Sarai, Abram's wife had borne him no children. But she had an Egyptian servant named Hagar; so she said to Abram, "The Lord has kept me from having children. Go, sleep with my servant; perhaps I can build a family through her." Abram agreed to what Sarai said. So after Abram had been living in Canaan ten years, Sarai his wife took her Egyptian servant Hagar and gave her to her husband to be his wife. He slept with Hagar, and she conceived. When she knew she was pregnant, she began to despise her mistress. Then Sarai said to Abram, "You are responsible for the wrong I am suffering. I put my servant in your arms, and now that she knows she is pregnant, she despises me. May the* Lord *judge between you and me." "Your servant is in your hands," Abram said. "Do with her whatever you think best." Then Sarai mistreated Hagar; so she fled from her* (Genesis 16.1-6).

The above relationship had a wrong beginning, wrong motive, and a bad outside influence. Sarai was not able to have children. Maybe after ten years of waiting she and Abraham became impatient and thought that God had forgotten them. Sarai was selfish and acting out of her emotions. Like many of us sometimes do. She was concerned with building a family and not with God's ultimate purpose. You can't really blame Sarai and Abraham because if you had lived during their time period you might have done the same. There was almost nothing worse for a couple than to not bear a child, especially a male child. Sarai wanted to save herself from the worst possible shame of not having a son to be born in her household.

Now, I have a question for you. Why do you want to be married? Is it because God has ordained it for you? Is it for sexual fulfillment or a false sense of security? Is it so that you would no longer have to hear everyone ask the question, why aren't you married yet? I remember one time I had a relative ask me that question and then they added to the end of it: you aren't *funny* are you? You know what they mean by that, don't you? In other words, are you attracted to women instead of men? I had had enough. I could not do anything but laugh because it was totally shocking to hear that just because I had not gotten married I must be gay. There could be a number of other reasons why you want to help God out. Well, let me tell you now one time, two times and as many times as you need to hear it: God *doesn't* need your help. Perhaps your attitude is similar to Sarai's.

Hagar didn't have a choice in the matter. As you look at this relationship you see that Sarai was out of place and trying to play like a little god. Abram yielded to her decision instead of consulting with God. He should have been reminded of God's promise. He and Sarai should have come into agreement to pray for God's direction concerning the idea of giving Hagar to Abram. How quickly we forget the promises that God has given us when the fire is intensified or when persecution or shame comes. What do you expect God to do for you? Do you have it written down? Are you meditating upon it? Are you planning your work and working your plan daily? If you are not doing this, then how do you know where you are going and how will you recognize when you are there? Habakkuk 2.2 *makes it plain.* "Then the LORD replied: "Write down the revelation and make it plain on tablets so that a herald (whoever reads it) may run with it."

Do you know who called you to salvation and to a life of purpose? God did! He called you out of darkness into his marvelous light (Acts 26:18). The Message Bible says this beautifully. "I'm sending you off to open the eyes of the outsiders so they can see the difference between dark and light, and choose light, see the difference between Satan and God, and choose God. I'm sending you off to present my offer of sins forgiven, and a place in the family, inviting them into the company of those who begin real living by believing in me." God would not waste his time to call you if he did not have a plan and a purpose for your life. He is faithful. He is Spirit and Truth. Therefore, he has to be full of faithfulness. It is documented in I Thessalonians 5:24, "The one who calls you is faithful, and he will do it."

Chapter 3
God's Joy, Your Strength

The LORD is my strength and my shield; my heart trusts in him, and he helps me. My heart leaps for joy, and with my song I praise him.-
Psalm 28.7

My first name is Daisy, though over two years ago I purposefully chose to start using my middle name, Yvonne. In the past, every time I introduced myself as *Daisy* I smiled, which seemed to happen naturally. I almost never failed to get the following comment or a similar one. "Wow! What a beautiful name and it reminds me of sunshine, and it suits you so well." Of course, when I got that kind of comment I couldn't help but to keep smiling.

On a further note, I have had several people say don't ever stop smiling or lose your joy because it is a blessing to many people. That is encouraging; however, on a kind of negative note, let me tell you about an interesting situation. After church one Sunday as we were all leaving, suddenly this woman came out of nowhere and said something that I will never forget. She said, "Why are you so happy? I know you must have problems and everything is not perfect in your life." Okay? I could not do anything but stand in silence and guess what, "I kept smiling." It was just natural.

Why do I say all this? Well, I want to talk about joy. The Bible says that the joy of the Lord is our strength. So the reason why I was so strong was because of God's strength. In contrast, the woman that was questioning my joy might have not had joy because she was trying to live daily in her own strength, not Gods. Let's take a look at some scriptures. Joy is mentioned throughout the Bible.

Merriam-Webster's dictionary has one definition of joy that is simple and to the point: "a source or cause of delight." So you see joy can be a source or it can be what is caused by the source, seemingly one and the same. As a Christian, our source and cause of joy should be Jesus. Another person can not bring us joy. Material things and wealth can not bring us joy. Education can not bring us joy. Job success can not bring us joy. Believe me; I have experienced all of this to some measure. Let me say this. All these things can bring us happiness.

Notice that happiness is temporary and circumstantial, but joy can be permanent regardless of how things are going on in your life. If you were a person of the opposite sex, would you be more attracted to someone who is continually joyful, or someone who is moody, depending upon the circumstances in his or her life? You would choose the person who is joyful of course. What does joy tell you about them? It says they are content internally, though not necessarily satisfied with all of their personal circumstances.

Okay, let's look at some scriptures. *I Samuel 18.6* says, "When the men had returned home after David had killed the Philistine, the women came out from all the towns of Israel to meet King Saul with singing and dancing, with joyful songs and with timbrels and lyres." The men came home and the women met them pouting, complaining, and criticizing by asking what took so long and why they did not bring this and that. No, of course not, and if that were the case, I don't believe the men would be coming home. They would go as far from home as they could. The women were joyful and glad to see the men back from fighting. I bet their joy was so contagious that the men became joyful too.

Have you ever been around someone when you were not feeling your best, but they were so joyful that somehow your attitude and mood changed? Why? Joy is contagious. I don't apologize for using myself as an illustration because I know about me more than I know about anyone else on earth. Sometimes I ask people why they like to be around me. I am just curious, you know, especially concerning those whom you really don't have much in common with. You know what many of them have said. They said, "I like to be around you because you make me happy." They didn't use the word joy, but I understand what they meant. No one wants to be around a sad, complaining person, male or female, family or stranger. Joy is contagious!

Have I always been joyful? I wish I could say yes. I have been mostly joyful after experiencing the love of Christ, but several years ago I went through a battle with a deep depression, even to the point of thinking it would be better if I were not alive. God had given me dreams, visions and promises that just were not coming to pass. Yes, one of them involved him sending me a mate, but that really did not seem like it was ever going to come to pass. The depression seemingly happened suddenly, but in retrospect, I started slipping slowly, by not fellowshipping with the saints, feeling rejected and persecuted. I had opened the door for the accusation and the curse of the enemy, Satan. I was just focusing on the negative things in my life. I was not other centered at that time, but self-centered. This led me to not praying or reading the word of God as I should. I want to encourage you in your faith that whatever you do keep fellowship with other believers, pray and read your Bible. Meeting with the saints is very important because there could be times when you don't have enough strength or desire to pray or read the word. There are many scriptures that talk about the importance of Christian fellowship and encouraging one another.

Relationship Analysis
A Woman and Man Full of Joy
Ruth/Boaz

"**B**oaz asked the overseers of his harvesters, "Who does that young woman belong to?" The overseer replied, "She is the Moabite who came back from Moab with Naomi. She said, 'Please let me glean and gather among the sheaves behind the harvesters.' She came into the field and has remained here from morning till now, except for a short rest in the shelter.

So Boaz said to Ruth, "My daughter, listen to me. Don't go and glean in another field and don't go away from here. Stay here with the women who work for me. Watch the field where the harvesters are working, and follow along after the women. I have told the men not to lay a hand on you. And whenever you are thirsty, go and get a drink from the water jars the men have filled." At this she bowed down with her face to the ground.

She asked him, "Why have I found such favor in your eyes that you notice me-a foreigner?" Boaz replied, "I've been told all about what you have done for your mother-in-law since the death of your husband-how you left your father and mother and your homeland and came to live with a people you did not know before. May the *Lord* repay you for what you have done. May you be richly rewarded by the *Lord*, the God of Israel, under whose wings you have come to take refuge." "May I continue to find favor in your eyes, my Lord, she said. "You have reassured me and have spoken kindly to your servant-though I do not have the standing of one of your servants."

At mealtime Boaz said to her, "Come over here. Have some bread and dip it into the wine vinegar." When she sat down with the harvesters, he offered her some roasted grain. She ate all she wanted and had some left over. As she got up to glean, Boaz gave orders to his men, "Let her gather among the sheaves and don't reprimand her. Even pull out some stalks for her from the bundles and leave them for her to pick up, and don't rebuke her." .... Her mother-in-law asked her, "Where did you glean today? Where did you work? Blessed be the man who took notice of you!" Then Ruth told her mother-in-law about the one at whose place she had been working.

"The name of the man I worked with today is Boaz," she said. "The *Lord* bless him! Naomi said to her daughter-in-law. He has not stopped showing his kindness to the living and the dead." She added, "That man is our close relative; he is one of our family guardians." Then Ruth the Moabite said, "He even said to me, 'Stay with my workers until they finish harvesting all my grain.'" (Ruth 2.5-16, 19-21)

After having read this story, I believe that Ruth, Naomi and Boaz were full of joy. They saw something exciting on the horizon. Ruth and Naomi would not be shamed because Ruth had a potential husband. Naomi could have some grandchildren and wealth. In addition Boaz would get a hard working and non-complaining wife. Being joyful and having a pleasant, positive attitude is good for not only you, but everyone around you. I want also to point out the fact that Ruth was busy using her skills and making a life for herself. Then along came Boaz and took notice of her and would not let her out of his sight or to leave his place of business. Men, let me give you some advice. When you see a lady that you are attracted to who is healthy and full of the joy of the Lord you should not hesitate to approach her and let her know that you are really, really interested in getting to know her. And ladies, you need to be busy doing something with all your heart and let your beautiful inner spirit come forth to the outside to bring that glow of joy that attracts the right one for you.

Chapter 4
Peace Beyond Your Understanding

And the peace of God, which transcends all understanding,
will guard your hearts and your minds in Christ Jesus.
- Philippians 4.7

One of the greatest benefits of being in the Kingdom of God is that he gives us his peace. I don't know about you, but there have been times in my life when I knew that if it had not been for the peace of God I might have been living in the institution, constantly looking at the men and the women in the white jackets. I would have had a nervous break down. Those of us who have experienced a life without peace, which is probably most of us at some time or other, know that having the peace of God is definitely something that no one should be without.

The scripture in Philippians 4.7 states God's peace goes beyond our understanding and it will *keep* our hearts and minds. God's peace has a keeping power. Maybe you are one of those singles who have been asking "why God why" is it taking you so long? You have been praying for your mate for many years. But God either doesn't answer or he tells you that your mate is coming soon.

But *soon* you realize means something totally different for you and God. *2 Peter 3:8* says, "But do not forget this one thing, dear friends: With the Lord a day is like a thousand years, and a thousand years are like a day." A thousand years in your sight are like a day that has just gone by, or like a watch in the night. *(Psalm 90.4)* God's soon could mean *as soon as* you obey me, take care of some weak areas in your life, or become more mature in any number of ways. Or it could just be the way that God has chosen to teach you patience and self control through his specifically designed plan and path just for you. Sometimes you just don't know why God makes you wait, or why he never gives you that partner.

In Harper's Bible Dictionary it gives us the information that peace in the Old Testament Hebrew is 'Shalom' and its overall meaning *is wholeness or well-being.* If you look at it's meaning in the New Testament Greek language then it is simply the *absence of war and conflict.* Are you whole? Are you experiencing well-being? Is your life free of war and conflict? Now, for those of you who eventually want to move past singleness and toward a life of marriage then let me ask you something. Do you want a marriage that is whole? Do you want a marriage that continuously experiences well-being? Do you want a marriage free of war and conflict? If your answer is yes then here is the solution. You must become whole, continually experience well-being, and live each day free from war and conflict. Why? There are two reasons that I want to bring up. You are one of the two marriage partners, so if you don't have it together then your marriage is already headed toward the valley. Secondly, if you don't become like the one that you want to marry then how will you recognize a whole, peaceful, well being (human) when you see him or her? Selah! Now, I wouldn't give you all this information and leave you hanging, or at a stand still. How can you get this peace? Only God can give it to you and it comes through the sacrificial life of his son Jesus.

In *Leviticus 26.6,* God says, "I will grant peace in the land, and you will lie down, and no one will make you afraid..." My dear friends, I want to tell you to not just lie down, but close your eyes, and shut off your mind and sleep. There is no need for you to stay awake at night worrying about your future marriage or current state of singleness. If God is awake 24 hours a day, 7 days a week, then he doesn't need our help in watching over things. There is only one God and his name is *Lord.* Lord means that he is in control of everything!

Psalm 121 encourages us with the following verses: "I lift up my eyes to the mountains-where does my help come from? My help comes from the *Lord*, the Maker of heaven and earth. He will not let your foot slip-he who watches over you will not slumber; indeed, he who watches over Israel will neither slumber nor sleep. The *Lord* watches over you-the Lord is your shade at your right hand; the sun will not harm you by day, nor the moon by night. The *Lord* will keep you from all harm-he will watch over your life; the Lord will watch over your coming and going both now and forevermore." The Lord gives strength to his people; the Lord blesses his people with peace. (Psalm 29.11) I will listen to what God the Lord says; he promises peace to his people, his faithful servants-... (Psalm 85.8) Lord, you establish peace for us; all that you have accomplished you have done for us. (Isaiah 26.12)

Relationship Analysis
Attracted to a Manipulator and a Deceiver
Samson and Delilah

———⚬ꙮ⚬———

The Woman in the Valley

In *Judges 16.4-22* we will look at the classic story of Samson and Delilah. I am sure you have heard of it. Here it goes. "Some time later, he fell in love with a woman in the Valley of Sorek whose name was Delilah. The rulers of the Philistines went to her and said, 'See if you can lure him into showing you the secret of his great strength and how you can overpower him so you may tie him up and subdue him. Each one of us will give you eleven hundred shekels of silver.'

So Delilah said to Samson, 'Tell me the secret of your great strength and how you can be tied up and subdued.' Samson answered her, 'If anyone ties me with seven fresh thongs that have not been dried, I'll become as weak as any other man.' Then the rulers of the Philistines brought her seven fresh thongs that had not been dried, and she tied him with them. With men hidden in the room, she called to him, 'Samson, the Philistines are upon you!' But he snapped the thongs as easily as a piece of string snaps when it comes close to a flame. So the secret of his strength was not discovered.

Then Delilah said to Samson, 'You have made a fool of me; you lied to me. Come now, tell me how you can be tied.' He said, 'If anyone ties me securely with new ropes that have never been used, I'll become as weak as any other man.' So Delilah took new ropes and tied him with them. Then, with men hidden in the room, she called to him, 'Samson, the Philistines are upon you!' But he snapped the ropes off his arms as if they were threads. Delilah said to Samson, 'Until now you have been making a fool of me and lying to me. Tell me how you can be tied.'

He replied, 'If you weave the seven braids of my head, wove them into the fabric [the loom] and tighten it with the pin, I'll become as weak as any other man. So while he was sleeping, Delilah took the seven braids of his head, wove them into the fabric, and tightened it with the pin. Again, she called to him, 'Samson, the Philistines are upon you!' He awoke from his sleep and pulled up the pin and the loom, with the fabric. Then she said to him, 'How can you say, 'I love you,' when you won't confide in me?' 'This is the third time that you have made a fool of me and haven't told me the secret of your great strength.' With such nagging she prodded him day after day until he was tired to death. So he told her everything. 'No razor has ever been used on my head,' he said, 'because I have been a Nazarite dedicated to God from my mother's womb. If my head were shaved, my strength would leave me, and I would become as weak as any other man.'

When Delilah saw that he had told her everything, she sent word to the rulers of the Philistines, 'Come back once more; he has told me everything.' So the rulers of the Philistines returned with the silver in their hands. Having put him to sleep on her lap, she called for someone to shave off the seven braids of his hair, and so began to subdue him. And so his strength left him. Then she called, 'Samson, the Philistines are upon you!' He awoke from his sleep and thought, 'I'll go out as before and shake myself free.' But he did not know that the *Lord* had left him. Then the Philistines seized him, gouged out his eyes and took him down to Gaza. Binding him with bronze shackles, they set him to grinding grain in the prison. But the hair on his head began to grow again after he had been shaved."

Samson was a mighty man of God, but he liked to play with fire and he got burned. He fell in love while in the valley, which is the low place in life. The valley is a place where you don't have the peace of God. Symbolically, this could be emotionally, mentally, or financially. Samson was literally in the Valley of Sorek, but also he was in his own spiritual valley because he was not following the *Lord*.

When in the valley you have to make sure you are in tune with God because the power of the enemy is increased when you are in that low place. Maybe you got to that low place because you yielded to the enemy knowingly or through his subtle tactics. Discernment is low when you are in the valley as you can see in Samson's story. One of Samson's weaknesses, as I see it from the scriptures, was with women. He was also a habitual lier because of his continually giving Delilah wrong information concerning where his strength came from. In addition to that, he was playing games with her, but remembers he got burned with his own game. Delilah was enticing Samson and either he did not know it, which would seem a bit hard to believe since she did it many times and quite directly, or he didn't care because he wanted her more. When you are not operating in obedience, then your spiritual discernment is blocked. Maybe Samson had discernment, but he chose to ignore this prompting because his desire for Delilah was greater. Personally, I think he chose to ignore it and had become a bit conceited because of his strength. He didn't know defeat and he couldn't even envision the end of himself and his strength. Sounds like a little too much pride, right?

Delilah was also very dishonest. She was full of lust and sensuality. Her name means delightful, so she was a physically beautiful woman. There was no trust in the relationship. Here is a little point for men. You should avoid a nagging and controlling woman because she could cause you to do ungodly things. A person that is worldly or materialistic could possibly lead you out of God's will if you are not keen to the situation. The enemy will strip you and put you in bondage, if you do not know who your God is, or fail to hearken to his guidance.

The sad thing is that Samson woke up not realizing that God was no longer with him. I believe that is how the enemy operates mostly, slowly over time, and suddenly you find yourself out of God's will and not knowing he has left you. This is a very dangerous place to be. How many people today are operating in the name of the Lord, but the Lord left them a long time ago. Do you remember King Saul? Ouch! How do you get to know God initially anyway? First of all through an intimate, personal relationship and fellowship with him, through fellowshipping with other believers, praying, reading and studying the Bible. Is God still with you or has he left, as he did with Samson? If you are not obedient to God, and you refuse to obey him, God may take his favor and blessing from you. Always remember though that he is always standing and waiting for you to return to him but with a surrendered heart and will.

Chapter 5
Exchanging Kindness for Bitterness

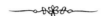

But when the kindness and love of God our Savior appeared, he saved us, not because of righteous things you had done, but because of his mercy
-Titus 3:4-5

There are many opportunities that God and life's circumstances give us that we could repay evil for evil. Of course, this is not the Lord's way, but it is the world's way of doing things. I think kindness is a fruit that does come more naturally for some and I don't know why it is like this. Perhaps some have had an easy life and haven't had lots of opportunity to develop a stony heart. It could be that it is their overall temperament and personality.

Kind people are easy to notice in public or anytime they come into your presence. These people usually have none-threatening facial expressions, often with a smile or as if they are about to smile at any moment and you can sense the sweetness of their spirit. They often are the first ones to apologize or to offer thanks and appreciation for something that you have done. Kindness is also shown through those who are quick to listen and slow to offer unsolicited advice.

With that said, if you go to the other extreme a person who is bitter is not difficult to spot either. The signs of bitterness are normally a sad or angry looking countenance, sometimes with a frown that stays on their face as if it were permanent make up. Sometimes people who are in deep bitterness can have a happy countenance because they have learned to cover their bitterness or might not even know that they have this deep seed that started with anger. When they speak it pierces negatively to the soul and sometimes damages beyond repair emotionally. Bitter people almost never have anything kind to say and if they do say something everyone is totally surprised that the nice comment came from *that* person. But usually it is a kind of kindness with a slant, meaning a negative comment often follows.

How does this relate to your singleness right now? Well, if you don't develop this fruit then you might remain single indefinitely. Who wants to be married to someone whose presence gives off the scent of "bitterness?" When I think of the word bitterness it leaves a nasty taste in my mouth, like lemons, vinegar or horseradish. It is not easy to get rid of a bitter or sour taste or foul scent? When you are checking someone out for a possible spouse you want to make sure that his or her words and deeds are full of kindness and sweetness. If you want to have words and an aroma that is sweet then you must first go to the sweetening agent-the Word of God. *Psalm 19:9-11* says, "The fear of the Lord is pure, enduring forever. The ordinances of the Lord are sure, and all of them are righteous. They are more precious than gold, than much pure gold; they are sweeter than honey, than honey from the honeycomb. By them your servant is warned; in keeping them there is great reward." Here is an example of how it should be in a romantic relationship-overflowing with sweetness. In the following case the man is speaking kind words about his lover. "*My dove in the clefts of the rock, in the hiding places on the mountainside, show me your face, let me hear your voice; for your voice is sweet and your face is lovely.*" (Song of Solomon 2.14)

Relationship Analysis
Run; Do Not Give Satan the Victory
Joseph and Potipher's Wife

———o❀❀o———

One of my favorite stories in the Scripture is that of Joseph whose brothers sold him into slavery, but when Israel (Jacob) died Joseph showed them kindness when, in my opinion, he had every right to give them what they deserved. Notice I said in my opinion, not what should be done according to the Word of God. In this case my opinion would be one according to the flesh and not the spirit.

Genesis 37.3-11 says, "Now Israel loved Joseph more than any of his other sons, because he had been born to him in his old age; and he made a richly ornamented robe for him. When his brothers saw that their father loved him more than any of them, they hated him and could not speak a kind word to him. Joseph had a dream, and when he told it to his brothers, they hated him all the more. He said to them, "Listen to this dream I had: You were binding sheaves of grain out in the field when suddenly my sheaf rose and stood upright, while your sheaves gathered around mine and bowed down to it." His brothers said to him, "Do you intend to reign over us? Will you actually rule us?" And they hated him all the more because of his dream and what he had said. Then he had another dream, and he told it to his brothers. "Listen," he said, "I had another dream, and this time the sun and the moon and the eleven stars were bowing down to me." When he told his father as well as his brothers, his father rebuked him and said, "What is this dream that you had? Will your mother and I and your actual brothers actually come and bow down to the ground before you?"

His brothers were jealous of him, but his father kept the matter in mind. Joseph's brothers were out grazing the family's sheep and Jacob sent Joseph out to look for them and take them some food, but Joseph's life would be changed forever and he would never come back to that particular home. If you follow me carefully you will see that this man was full of God's love and compassion because he had the authority to do whatever he wanted and it would be honored

Let us pick the story up again at *Genesis 37.19*. " 'Here comes that dreamer!" they said to each other. "Come now, let's kill him and throw him into one of these cisterns and say that a ferocious animal devoured him. Then we will see what comes of his dreams.'... (v. 26) Judah said to his brothers, 'What will we gain if we kill our brother and cover up his blood? Come, let's sell him to the Ishmaelites and not lay our hands on him; after all, he is our brother, our own flesh and blood.' His brothers agreed….(v.28) So when the Midianite merchants came by, his brothers pulled Joseph up out of the cistern and sold him for twenty shekels of silver to the Ishmaelites, who took him to Egypt. (v. 34) Then Jacob tore his clothes, put on sackcloth, and mourned for his son many days…..

So as time passed Joseph was put in charge of Potipher's household and all that he owned, but Potipher's wife found Joseph very attractive and she wanted to sleep with him. Potipher was one of Pharaoh's officials. When Joseph refused her proposition, she lied and made it look like Joseph tried to rape her and this landed him in prison.

But God was with Joseph and he had favor and prosperity, even in prison. *So Pharaoh sent for Joseph, and he was quickly brought from the dungeon. When he had shaved and changed his clothes he came before Pharaoh. Pharaoh said to Joseph, I had a dream, and no one can interpret it. But I have heard it said of you that when you hear a dream you can interpret it.* (Genesis 41. 14,15) Joseph did interpret the dream and was made second in command in all of Egypt. The interpretation of the dream was that there was going to be seven years of abundance and seven years of plenty. The key was to store up in the time of abundance so that there would be food in famine. Joseph had the plan for this and when the famine came it was severe and had an effect on the world at that time, including Joseph's family's hometown. Israel sent Joseph's brothers to Egypt to buy food and they bowed down to Joseph though they did not recognize him, but he most definitely recognized them. You should read this entire story in detail and it will fascinate you.

But the point I want to get to is that Joseph could have been very bitter toward them, but instead he was full of the fruit of Kindness. *"When Joseph's brothers saw that their father was dead, they said, 'What if Joseph holds a grudge against us and pays us back for all the wrong things we did to him?' So they sent word to Joseph, saying, 'Your father left these instructions before he died: 'This is what you are to say to Joseph: I ask you to forgive your brothers the sins and wrongs they committed in treating you so badly.' Now please forgive the sins of the servants of the God of your father.' When their message came to him, Joseph wept. His brothers then came and threw themselves down before him. 'We are your slaves,' they said. But Joseph said to them, 'Don't be afraid. Am I in the place of God? You intended to harm me, but God intended it for good to accomplish what is now being done, the saving of many lives. So then, don't be afraid. I will provide for you and your children.' And he reassured them and spoke kindly to them."* (Genesis 50.15-21)

As you can see from these scriptures, Joseph in the natural had the right to do whatever he wanted to with his brothers, but he was a kind person and he forgave them. But rest assured the dreamer's dream came true as his brothers bowed down before him many times. You must be careful how you treat others that God allow in your lives, including your families because you never know what God has planned for them and you don't want to be at odds with anyone. As the Bible tells us we are to love everyone and owe no man anything. How does this relate to singles? Well, just like it applies to everyone. If you want to be loved, you first must show yourself to be loveable. Would you rather be around someone who shows loving care for you or someone who really doesn't care if you are in their lives or not? Of course, we want to be around people who celebrate us, not tolerate us as I have heard often said. Let us continually let our tongues speak words of kindness and our hands ready to do righteous acts of kindness.

Chapter 6
Desire Goodness in Everything

—∽◈∾—

"With this in mind, we constantly pray for you, that our God may make you worthy of his calling, and that by his power he may bring to fruition your every desire for goodness and your every deed prompted by faith.
-2 Thessalonians 1.11

How many of you have ever been around someone who always has something negative to say about someone or a situation? Maybe you yourself have once been this person. If you are this kind of person right now, could this be the reason when you start talking to people they suddenly have to go or are suddenly busy? Because when someone is constantly being negative and saying bad things about people or a situation it can be very draining and depressing. I have been in both positions-one who has been on the receiving and unfortunately the giving end. And I must confess that I don't like any one of those.

But what I do like is to have my life full of goodness both as a receiver and giver. That is what God desires for all of his children. In the scripture for this chapter it lets us know that God wants goodness to be a part of our life and he wants our life to be one of faith. I see many times people give good things or do good things, but with the wrong motives. They might want others to see them, say something nice about them or expect something in return for their efforts. That is the wrong kind of attitude and I believe most of us would rather they keep their gifts than be entangled with this yoke of bondage. And that is exactly what it is-a yoke.

Whenever you can not give or receive freely then that is a yoke. In *2 Thessalonians 1.11* the writer says that goodness only comes through the power of God and goodness will make us worthy to be called believers. It says that he will make come to pass even our desire for goodness. You don't even have to be doing anything good yet, but just desire it. He looks at your heart and through your desires and faith God will bring all the goodness out of it so that others will receive their blessings. As believers, whether single or married, you are to desire goodness in everything. Yes, even when it is to your disadvantage or has no effect upon you at all. For example, as a single, how many times have you seen the Lord bless one of your relatives, church members, co-workers, friends or acquaintances with a marriage partner? Granted, some of these are not blessings and those who are in the marriage will later be able to testify to this when it seems like all hell has broken loose. But the Bible tells us to rejoice with those who rejoice. I truly believe that when I am honestly happy for another's happiness then my blessing is not far off. God is able to make all grace abound until it is your time to say, "I do." What effect does someone with goodness have on their life and other's lives? The immediate effect might be surprise and happiness, but as a Christian the long term effect will hopefully be to point them in the direction of God.

Only God can use you to bring change when it comes from a heart flowing with faith, hope and love. There is also a positive result for the giver of goodness. Can you guess what that is? It is that the more you give, the more God gives to you and the more that you want to give. Hey singles! You never know if Boaz, meaning the right one for you, is watching from a distance and your goodness can draw him closer because he wants to get a better picture of who the person is behind all of this goodness. Remember don't give goodness because of your low self esteem, insecurities or pride, but give goodness because you just can't help yourself. It is part of your Christian character.

Relationship Analysis I
Goodness is Full of Surprises
Moses and Zipporah

L et us take a look at two relationships where we can see the goodness of God. First, is the relationship of Moses and Zipporah. Many of you probably know the story of Moses and how he was put in the Nile River in a reed basket as an infant and Pharaoh's daughter took him and raised him as her own child. He was very educated and had many material things, not only everything that he needed, but probably everything that he desired. God had made Moses a deliverer and one day he saw a fight between an Egyptian and an Israelite and being the deliverer that he was he killed the Egyptian.

When Pharaoh heard of this, he tried to kill Moses, but Moses fled from Pharaoh and went to live in Midian, where he sat down by a well. Now a priest of Midian had seven daughters, and they came to draw water and fill the troughs to water their father's flock. Some shepherds came along and drove them away, but Moses got up and came to their rescue and watered their flock. When the girls returned to Reuel their father, he asked them, "Why have you returned so early today? They answered, "An Egyptian rescued us from the shepherds. He even drew water for us and watered the flock. "And where is he?" he asked his daughters. "Why did you leave him? Invite him to have something to eat." Moses agreed to stay with the man, who gave his daughter Zipporah to Moses in marriage. Zipporah gave birth to a son, and Moses named him Gershom, saying, "I have become a foreigner in a foreign land." (Exodus 2.15-22)

Moses had to leave the place that he had known as home suddenly. Looking at the situation, I am sure he did not have the luxury of packing and planning for the move. Sometimes in our lives we also have to make sudden choices, but they are God directed. Though Moses had to run suddenly, God was still with him as always. Not only was he able to immediately get another job as a shepherd, but he met a beautiful, single woman named Zipporah whose father was very wise. God was good to Moses. And to top that, he fathered several sons. That is only the beginning of the story. You will have to read the book of Exodus for yourself to see what I am talking about. Surely, his goodness and mercy lasts forever.

Relationship Analysis II
Goodness is Full of Surprises
Hosea and Gomer

The second relationship that I would like to look at is that of Hosea, the prophet and Gomer, the prostitute. Interesting combination, huh? Only God could do that and not be condemned. *When the Lord began to speak through Hosea, the LORD said to him, "Go, marry a promiscuous woman and have children with her, for like an adulterous wife this land is guilty of unfaithfulness to the LORD." So he married Gomer daughter of Diblaim, and she conceived and bore him a son.* (Hosea 1.2,3) I would definitely say that God showed his goodness to Gomer who had lived an unholy life and most assuredly a surprise for Hosea the prophet of God. If a minister today would marry someone whom the church thinks is not the right "material," I wonder how that would go over. Selah!

He was going to marry someone whose life was in direct opposition to what he prophesied and whom he represented-holiness and God. God was good to them because he opened Gomer's womb two times afterwards and she gave birth to a daughter and another son. God was good to them. How do you apply this to your life today? Sometimes you know you don't deserve the blessings of God because of your rebellion and unfaithfulness to God, but all you have to do is repent and the Lord Jesus will give you a second chance. That is what his grace is about. If it had not been for the Lord on our side where would we be right now? (Psalm 124.1-8) Surely goodness and mercy shall follow you all the days of your life. (Psalm 23.6)

Chapter 7
Faithfulness Is Not Short Term

For great is his love toward us, and the *faithfulness*
of the Lord endures forever. Praise the Lord
-Psalm 117.2

When I think of the word faithfulness, of course, I see the base word of faith, which to me means total belief in something. In this case I see it as total belief in God. When I have faith in God there is no space left for doubt. I will give you a visual. Think about a glass of water. If you fill the class up 25%, 50% or 75% then there is still space. This extra space could be seen as doubt. But if you fill the glass up all the way to the tip then there will be no space left for air or anything. That glass would be full of faith. This reminds me of times when God's faith comes upon me and leaves no room for doubt.

There is a well-known Christian song that has as one of its main lines, "This is the air I breathe." God has shown me that he wants our faith to be like the air that we breathe. We don't think about the next second of breath that we are going to take because it is automatic. We never give it a second thought unless we start doing some kind of strenuous exercise and we become short of breath. Could you imagine how life would be if we had our faith so stirred up that we do not even think twice when the Holy Spirit gives us direction to do something? We do not continually ask God for air to breathe, but if we are grateful, hopefully we are thanking him for the gift of breath, at least occasionally. God wants you to depend upon him for your *daily* provision, even though you have planned in advance for months or years. The more I think about it, I believe God gives us big dreams and plans so that we will not be able to depend upon ourselves or our talents to make it happen, nor will we be able to pat ourselves on our backs when it does come to pass.

What are the big dreams that God has given you that seem not come to pass? Perhaps it is not your, "for such a time as this" moment. When it is time, you and everyone will know and God will grant you favor and provision. *Keep pressing on and most importantly keep listening for his voice and obey each direction that he gives.*

Are you faithful and other-centered with your family, friends, co-workers and the local church or fellowship group you are a part of? Are you being committed to your church or fellowship group and the things that you volunteered to do? God is watching whether you think he is or not. God's faithfulness to you endures forever as you can see in *Psalm 117.2*, which says, "For great is his love toward us, and the faithfulness of the Lord endures forever. Praise the Lord."

In *Proverbs 3.3* it says, "Let love and faithfulness never leave you; bind them around your neck, write them on the tablet of your heart." In this scripture we see that God wants us married to faithfulness. In God's kind of covenant he expects eternal faithfulness without excuses. He wants faithfulness to him to be just as automatic as your reflex or your heart beat. God is faithful and he expects you to be faithful. He wouldn't ask you to do something that he himself would not do. It says it quite well in *Lamentations 3.23*, "They are new every morning; great is your faithfulness." Faithful could be one of God's names. When everyone else has rejected you or failed you, you can always count on him. Even if you become unfaithful, God is so good that he still remains faithful. *(Romans 3.3)*

Relationship Analysis I
Faithfulness Lasts Forever
Ahasuerus and Esther

From Faithfulness to Queen

One of my most favorite Bible stories is the story of Esther. It is such an energetic and inviting text. I think it is every woman's dream to end up with the victory as Esther did with the title of Queen and with being able to complete such a God given task to save her people-the Jews from being annihilated. She had favor with the king, but after awhile things became shaky where the king did not trust her, but God intervened and restored her favor. *In the Lord's hand the king's heart is a stream of water that he channels toward all who please him.*(Proverbs 21.1) So from the following scripture you can see that Esther pleased the Lord and he found her faithful.

Esther 8.1-8 reads, "That same day King Xerxes gave Queen Esther the estate of Haman, the enemy of the Jews. And Mordecai came into the presence of the king, for Esther had told how he was related to her. The king took off his signet ring, which he had reclaimed from Haman, and presented it to Mordecai. And Esther appointed him over Haman's estate."

Esther again pleaded with the king, falling at his feet and weeping. She begged him to put an end to the evil plan of Haman the Agagite, which he had devised against the Jews. Then the king extended the gold scepter to Esther and she arose and stood before him. "If it pleases the king," she said, "and if he regards me with favor and thinks it the right thing to do, and if he is pleased with me, let an order be written overruling the dispatches that Haman son of Hammedatha, the Agagite, devised and wrote to destroy the Jews in all the king's provinces. For how can I bear to see disaster fall on my people? How can I bear to see the destruction of my family?"

King Xerxes replied to Queen Esther and to Mordecai the Jew, "Because Haman attacked the Jews, I have given his estate to Esther, and they have impaled him on the pole he set up. Now write another decree in the king's name in behalf of the Jews as seems best to you, and seal it with the king's signet ring-for no document written in the king's name and sealed with his ring can be revoked."

Relationship Analysis II
Faithfulness Lasts Forever
David and Michal

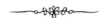

Faithfulness on the Way to the Purpose

Still there is another relationship I would like to look at. Though David's prize in the task that was put before him was a woman, this situation to me is more of looking at how God's faithfulness continued with David even though he was not in the office as king yet. Saul had been trying to get rid of-literally kill David, but God always protected David, his called and anointed one.

When you have God on your side no one can be against you. He is more than the whole world against you. That is scripture my friend. *I Samuel 18.20-29*, "Now Saul's daughter Michal was in love with David, and when they told Saul about it, he was pleased. "I will give her to him," he thought, "so that she may be a snare to him and so that the hand of the Philistines may be against him." So Saul said to David, "Now you have a second opportunity to become my son-in-law."

Then Saul ordered his attendants: "Speak to David privately and say, 'Look, the king likes you, and his attendants all love you; now become his son-in-law.' "They repeated these words to David. But David said, "Do you think it is a small matter to become the king's son-in-law? I'm only a poor man and little known."

When Saul's servants told him what David had said, Saul replied, "Say to David, 'The king wants no other price for the bride than a hundred Philistine foreskins, to take revenge on his enemies.' "Saul's plan was to have David fall by the hands of the Philistines. When the attendants told David these things, he was pleased to become the king's son-in-law. So before the allotted time elapsed, David took his men with him and went out and killed two hundred Philistines and brought back their foreskins. They counted out the full number to the king so that David might become the king's son-in-law.

Then Saul gave him his daughter Michal in marriage. When Saul realized that the Lord was with David and that his daughter Michal loved David, Saul became still more afraid of him, and he remained his enemy the rest of his days. The Philistine commanders continued to go out to battle, and as often as they did, David met with more success than the rest of Saul's officers, and his name became well known." God's faithfulness to David remained with him as you can see since God made David more successful in his battles than the rest of Saul's men and Saul knew that the hand of God was upon David whether he wanted to admit it or not. It is interesting that though Saul was in the office of king, God favored David over him. God looks at the hearts of his children and not titles or positions. Saul had evil intentions for David, but David always respected Saul's office as king and David passed up many opportunities to destroy Saul, of which he had the ability to do. God never left David and He will never leave you.

Chapter 8
Are You Wearing the
Garment of Gentleness?

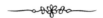

Let your *gentleness* be evident to all. The Lord is near-Philippians 4.5

I t is really easy to identify gentleness, isn't it? I believe even the most unspiritual person can pick out this fruit. Actually, I have known several non Christians who were very gentle people, sometimes even more so than some Christians, sad to say of course. Gentleness is similar to joy, it attracts like a magnet. People like to be around someone who is approachable and whom they can speak their minds freely and receive acceptance in return.

When I think of gentleness the picture of a puppy comes to my mind, but the most gentle of all animals would be a lamb. The Bible tells us that is how you should be. It all starts with God. When he speaks to us his Holy Spirit is gentle-a *gentleMAN. 1 Kings 19.11-13* says, "The Lord said, "Go out and stand on the mountain in the presence of the Lord, for the Lord is about to pass by." Then a great and powerful wind tore the mountains apart and shattered the rocks before the Lord, but the Lord was not in the wind. After the wind there was an earthquake, but the Lord was not in the earthquake. A fire came after the earthquake, but the Lord was not in the fire. And after the fire came a gentle whisper. When Elijah heard it, he pulled his cloak over his face and went out and stood at the mouth of the cave. Then a voice said to him, "What are you doing here, Elijah?" When you look at this you see that God did not come with a loud presence, though he had done that before and could do it again if he wanted to. But he was teaching Elijah, the prophet, a new sound, a new voice, a new way to hear him-in a *gentle* whisper.

You can get so busy sometimes that your lives become very noisy and it is difficult for you to hear what the Holy Spirit is saying to you because the loudness overwhelms the softness or gentleness of his voice. If you looked at the fruit as articles or pieces of clothing, then I believe every Christian needs to make sure to get this fruit as quickly as possible. Why? This is one of the major ways that Christians can be distinguished from unbelievers because there is so much self-centeredness in the world. People don't care about being gentle and sensitive in their demeanor and words. Yes, even men need to be gentle. Christ was the epitome of gentleness. Gentleness is very attractive as a fruit. When you are looking for a potential spouse you should see if they have developed this fruit. Gentleness would come in quite handy when those times of disagreements in your relationship happen. And they will happen, even with God fearing and loving Christians.

Relationship Analysis
Gentle as a Lamb
David and Abigail

———◦◦◦———

David Asks for Favor

Let us look at the *gentleness* of Abigail, who was wise and beautiful. Before she married David she was the wife of Nabal, a very wealthy man. She was able to spare her life by being gentle to the great warrior David. *I Samuel 25* begins with David sending some of his men to Nabal to give this message, "'Now I hear that it is sheep-shearing time. When your shepherds were with us, you did not mistreat them, and the whole time they were at Carmel nothing of theirs was missing. Ask your own servants and they will tell you. Therefore be favorable toward my men, since you come at a festive time. Please give your servants and your son David whatever you can find for them.'" The messengers received an answer from Nabal that did not set well with David.

In I Samuel 25.10-11 Nabal answered David's servants, "Who is this David? Who is this son of Jesse? Many servants are breaking away from their masters these days. Why should I take my bread and water, and the meat I have slaughtered for my shearers, and give it to men coming from who knows where?" Now I must give you the rest of the main scripture so you will understand how David fell in love with the gentleness of Abigail. *I Samuel 25.14-43* reads, "One of the servants told Abigail, Nabal's wife, "David sent messengers from the wilderness to give our master his greetings, but he hurled insults at them. Yet these men were very good to us. They did not mistreat us, and the whole time we were out in the fields near them nothing was missing. Night and day they were a wall around us the whole time we were herding our sheep near them. Now think it over and see what you can do, because disaster is hanging over our master and his whole household. He is such a wicked man that no one can talk to him."

"Abigail acted quickly. She took two hundred loaves of bread, two skins of wine, five dressed sheep, five seahs of roasted grain, a hundred cakes of raisins and two hundred cakes of pressed figs, and loaded them on donkeys. Then she told her servants, "Go on ahead; I'll follow you." But she did not tell her husband Nabal. As she came riding her donkey into a mountain ravine, there were David and his men descending toward her, and she met them.

David had just said, "It's been useless—all my watching over this fellow's property in the wilderness so that nothing of his was missing. He has paid me back evil for good. May God deal with David, be it ever so severely, if by morning I leave alive one male of all who belong to him!"

When Abigail saw David, she quickly got off her donkey and bowed down before David with her face to the ground. She fell at his feet and said: "Pardon your servant, my Lord, and let me speak to you; hear what your servant has to say. Please pay no attention, my Lord, to that wicked man Nabal. He is just like his name—his name means Fool, and folly goes with him. And as for me, your servant, I did not see the men my Lord sent. And now, my Lord, as surely as the LORD your God lives and as you live, since the LORD has kept you from bloodshed and from avenging yourself with your own hands, may your enemies and all who are intent on harming my Lord be like Nabal.

And let this gift, which your servant has brought to my Lord, be given to the men who follow you. "Please forgive your servant's presumption. The LORD your God will certainly make a lasting dynasty for my Lord, because you fight the LORD's battles, and no wrongdoing will be found in you as long as you live. Even though someone is pursuing you to take your life, the life of my Lord will be bound securely in the bundle of the living by the LORD your God, but the lives of your enemies he will hurl away as from the pocket of a sling. When the LORD has fulfilled for my Lord every good thing he promised concerning him and has appointed him ruler over Israel, my Lord will not have on his conscience the staggering burden of needless bloodshed or of having avenged himself. And when the LORD your God has brought my Lord success, remember your servant."

David said to Abigail, "Praise be to the LORD, the God of Israel, who has sent you today to meet me. May you be blessed for your good judgment and for keeping me from bloodshed this day and from avenging myself with my own hands. Otherwise, as surely as the LORD, the God of Israel, lives, who has kept me from harming you, if you had not come quickly to meet me, not one male belonging to Nabal would have been left alive by daybreak."

Then David accepted from her hand what she had brought him and said, "Go home in peace. I have heard your words and granted your request." When Abigail went to Nabal, he was in the house holding a banquet like that of a king. He was in high spirits and very drunk. So she told him nothing at all until daybreak. Then in the morning, when Nabal was sober, his wife told him all these things, and his heart failed him and he became like a stone.

About ten days later, the LORD struck Nabal and he died. When David heard that Nabal was dead, he said, "Praise be to the

LORD, who has upheld my cause against Nabal for treating me with contempt. He has kept his servant from doing wrong and has brought Nabal's wrongdoing down on his own head."

Then David sent word to Abigail, asking her to become his wife. His servants went to Carmel and said to Abigail, "David has sent us to you to take you to become his wife." She bowed down with her face to the ground and said, "I am your servant and am ready to serve you and wash the feet of my Lord's servants." Abigail quickly got on a donkey and, attended by her five female servants, went with David's messengers and became his wife.

Wow! Lots of scripture huh? Well, the Bible is full of God's wisdom. One thing that I really like about Abigail is that she was full of wisdom and was able to recognize where the hand of the LORD was. And I believe she knew it was upon David. She realized she had married a fool and she decided inwardly that she did not want a fool's reward. Perhaps to her being married to wealthy Nabal was nothing compared to choosing to follow the hand of the LORD. Also notice that Nabal and Abigail had some wise servants who realized the wisdom and gentleness of the master's wife Abigail so they decided that Nabal had responded incorrectly and they sought the wisdom of Abigail. They gave her the correct report about David and his men. In addition, they realized that not only Nabal would be doomed, but his whole household and that included them. She immediately sensed the wise thing to do and acted quickly. If you look at Abigail's response more closely then you will certainly realize that she was prophesying and was God's mouth piece. She had such confidence in David and the LORD. David received her gift of apology and sent her home in peace, but I tell you David did not waste anytime in asking Abigail to be his wife when he realized that Nabal was dead. She was full of gentleness. Gentleness is not something that can be hidden, but will be evident to all.

Chapter 9
God-Control, Not Self-Control

---∘♧∘---

Like a city whose walls are broken down is a man who lacks self-control
-Proverbs 25:28

When I look at the word self-control I see that it is really two words with separate meanings when they are alone. The words give a more specific meaning when they are made into a compound word. Let us look at them separately from Merriam-Webster's dictionary. First, let us look at self. An excellent definition is *"the union of elements (as body, emotions, thoughts, and sensations) that constitute the individuality and identity of a person."*

Our self is made up of our body, emotions, thoughts and sensations. Sensation is that which pertains to the senses. These things are what make us who we are. Now, let us look at control. The best definition is "to exercise restraining or directing influence over; to have power over." I was curious to see how Merriam-Webster defined the compound word *self-control*. It is excellent. *"Restraint exercised over one's own impulses, emotions, or desires."* To break it down even more, it is saying that the person is controlling his or her own impulses, emotions, or desires and you all know that it is next to impossible to do those ourselves through self-control, especially on a consistent basis.

We need help. Problems with self-control have been here from the beginning and we will look at two relationships later that had God-control. Do you remember earlier that I talked about Samson and Delilah? You could look at Samson as an example of someone who had self-control and not God-control.

In the Bible Paul gives us a good understanding of how self-control is a constant battle. There are different challenges for each individual person. Some might have problems with controlling their emotions, others with desire for food, others with compulsive shopping, still others with sexual promiscuity, and I am sure there are as many challenges as there are people. So I can't name them all here. Paul says in *Romans 7.15-25* (NIRV), "I don't understand what I do. I don't do what I want to do. Instead, I do what I hate to do. I do what I don't want to do. So I agree that the law is good. As it is, I am no longer the one who does these things. It is sin living in me that does them. I know there is nothing good in my sinful nature. I want to do what is good, but I can't. I don't do the good things I want to do. I keep on doing the evil things I don't want to do. I do what I don't want to do. But I am not really the one who is doing it. It is sin living in me. Here is the law I find working in me. When I want to do good, evil is right there with me. Deep inside me I find joy in God's law. But I see another law working in the parts of my body. It fights against the law of my mind. It makes me a prisoner of the law of sin. That law controls the parts of my body. What a terrible failure I am! Who will save me from this sin that brings death to my body? I give thanks to God. He will do it through Jesus Christ our Lord. So in my mind I am a slave to God's law. But in my sinful nature I am a slave to the law of sin."

As you can see even the great Apostle Paul had struggles in the flesh or with the carnal nature. It seems that his challenge was with the physical body-maybe sexual temptations, but sometimes you may have some struggles just as challenging to you. None of them can be controlled by self because of the sin that is in us, but we have to give it over to God and let him have control. In the scripture at the beginning of this chapter is *Proverbs 25.28* and it gives us a visual picture of someone without self control-male or female. Like a city whose walls are broken down, is a man who lacks self-control. I get the picture. Can you see the picture? I see a very large city that is an open field because there are no buildings or walls of protection. There is nothing keeping people or animals from going out or coming in, so I see total chaos. This is what the writer of Proverbs says happens to you when you have no self-control

Well, I have some good news for you. Though, it is impossible to control yourself, you can do it with the help of the Holy Spirit who is deposited in you as a Christian. And if you are not a Christian all is not lost, you can become a Christian. Ask God to forgive you of your sins and come into your heart. It is as simple as that. As a single, or even a married person if you happen to be reading this book, you need to ask for God's control and lay your self-control on the altar. Who wants to marry someone who is still full of self? I am not saying that God's control is going to be a piece of cake, no you will probably have to go through some times of testing to see if you really want to give up your control and take God's. The blessings of God await those of you who do decide to submit your control to God. Personally, I believe this fruit has been one of the most difficult for me to cultivate because of my independent spirit and having to be responsible for myself right after high school. I am not saying even now that I have arrived. I am still learning, but I do believe that the seed has been planted and I can begin to see what looks like fruit in this area. Paul reminds me that I must die daily.

Probably, one of the most difficult tests in the area of self-control to many, including myself in the past, has been in the area of submission to authority. Sometimes the boss can really put you through some tests because I believe God allows them to do that to those of you that he knows still need to be broken some more in this area. If the boss rubs you the wrong way no matter what job you find yourself at, then you might be in need of some God control in the area of submission to authority. Listen, I have been there, done that. Trust me, submit quickly and move on to greater things. I want to leave you with this encouraging scripture. *"Brothers and Sisters, may the grace of our Lord Jesus Christ be with your spirit. Amen."* (Galatians 6.18 NIRV)

Relationship Analysis I
God-Control
Joseph and Mary

—◦✦◦—

Other-Centeredness

How can you be able to know if someone is being God controlled or self controlled? It is very simple. Are they other centered? If you think about how you can make others happy and how you can please God through serving others then you are God controlled. If the Word of God is first place in your life and you desire to obey HIM above all else then you are God controlled. If it causes you great pain to be in sin, then you are God controlled. I think my point is clear now huh? Let us look at three people whom I admire.

The first are the couple who are the parents of our LORD and Saviour, Jesus Christ, which are Joseph and Mary. *Matthew 1.18-25* (NIRV) says, "This is how the birth of Jesus Christ came about. His mother Mary and Joseph had promised to get married. But before they started to live together, it became clear that she was going to have a baby. She became pregnant by the power of the Holy Spirit. Her husband Joseph was a godly man. He did not want to put her to shame in public. So he planned to divorce her quietly. But as Joseph was thinking about this, an angel of the Lord appeared to him in a dream. The angel said, "Joseph, son of David, don't be afraid to take Mary home as your wife. The baby inside her is from the Holy Spirit. She is going to have a son. You must give him the name Jesus. That is because he will save his people from their sins." All of this took place to bring about what the Lord had said would happen. He had said through the prophet, "The virgin is going to have a baby. She will give birth to a son. And he will be called Immanuel."-(Isaiah 7.14) The name Immanuel means "God with us." Joseph woke up. He did what the angel of the Lord commanded him to do. He took Mary home as his wife. But he did not make love to her until after she gave birth to a son. And Joseph gave him the name Jesus." Probably throughout all history this is the ideal couple in that you see that Joseph was so understanding, quick to forgive and immediately obeyed God's command.

Relationship Analysis II
God-Control
Joseph and Potipher's Wife

―⊶◈◈⊶―

Quick to Obey

How many of you can say that you are quick to obey? If you are in any way part of this world, then I would say that it is not easy for you to obey with all the worldly influences around you. Many of you have the desire to obey, but the desire to obey and actually obeying are totally two different things. Joseph could have been self-focused, yes, even after having had the visitation from the angel of the LORD. He had the option to believe the lie of the enemy of his mind and thoughts (self-controlled) or follow the direction of God's angel. ....*But for Adam no suitable helper was found. So the LORD God caused the man to fall into a deep sleep; and while he was sleeping, he took one of the man's ribs and then closed up the place with flesh. Then the LORD God made a woman from the rib he had taken out of the man, and he brought her to the man. The man said, "This is now bone of my bones and flesh of my flesh; she shall be called 'woman,' for she was taken out of man." For this reason a man will leave his father and mother and be united to his wife, and they will become one flesh.* Genesis 2:20-24

Could you be the one that is holding up God's marriage plans for you? If you honestly looked at yourself from an opposite sex perspective, what would turn you off? What could you improve about yourself? What do you have to give? All of us want to have high standards for future marriage partners, but do you meet the standards of the future partners? Please do not misunderstand me. I am primarily, but not totally speaking of spiritual maturity and the fruit of the Spirit.

In the singles group, which I founded a few years ago, I took a basic survey. Males and females were asked simple, yet very important questions. This survey was by no means final and was taken from a small sampling. But I believe it is a good measure of how singles feel in general, especially Christians. The questions pertained to what they liked in a potential mate. I am mentioning the most popular desires.

Women are looking for providers. Some women may not be honest about this. It is our very nature to have a man that can and will provide for us in many ways. I have a question for the men who desire marriage. Are you able to provide for a wife, yourself and perhaps children? If the answer is no then please make sure you tell her that before you marry, so she can decide if she wants to be a part of that while you are working on being more financially stable. This would usually mean that she will have to work as well. Otherwise, after the marriage ceremony you may be surprised when she refuses to work.

Men are looking for love and intimacy. And of course you know intimacy probably refers to sex right? They were perhaps being respectful in using the term intimacy I believe, especially since we were singles. This was somewhat a surprise. I thought this (intimacy) would be at the top of the female's list. Well, it did run a close second. Now, I will once again address the men. Are you willing to go through the process of developing a godly friendship? You will need to learn to care for the woman. If you give love, you will also receive love and intimacy. When I speak of intimacy before marriage I am not talking sex, but sharing the depths of ones' heart. This could possibly mean rejection and may step on your (the man's) ego and pride. But it would be worth it, because God could reveal things to strengthen your character in the process.

Sometimes the desires of Christian singles are to date those that are not born-again believers. Thus the question arises concerning the reason a Christian should marry another believer. God's word tells us that anything otherwise spells destruction. There is a lot of deception here. You can not change anyone. You can not make anyone become a Christian. A believer and a non-believer do not have a lot in common, so they cannot produce a God-led relationship. If they are quite compatible, the Christian could be carnal-minded. I am not saying that you should not talk to a non-believer. What I am saying is that the conversations, lifestyles and values of a non Christian are not in accordance with the word of God. You might be thinking of someone you know that is a good person, but they are not saved. They may be good, but if they are not saved, then they are not good enough for you. 2 Corinthians 6:14 says, *Do not be yoked together with unbelievers. For what do righteousness and wickedness have in common? Or what fellowship can light have with darkness?* There is another side to this as well.

As a Christian you could be dating another Christian and be unequally yoked. How can this be? One of you may be a young Christian or carnal-minded and the other may be spiritually-minded. Please be careful that you do not have a false sense of spirituality that you think you can change or remake someone after you are married to them. If you are involved in this type of relationship, it would not be a bad idea if you let your possible future mate mature and manifest some fruit of the Spirit before saying "I do." If the fruit is developed before your marriage, then it will be more fulfilling.

Nelson's Illustrated Bible Dictionary describes or defines marriage as "the union of a man and a woman as husband and wife, which becomes the foundation for a home and a family."

Man should not be alone. Women and men were made to be companions to each other. The man should know the type of companion that he needs, so he must go and find her. Proverbs 18:22 says, *He who finds a wife finds what is good and receives favor from the LORD.* In Genesis 2:18-23 you see that God made man, animals and last he made the woman. *"The LORD God said, "It is not good for the man to be alone. I will make a helper suitable for him." Now the LORD God had formed out of the ground all the wild animals and all the birds in the sky. He brought them to the man to see what he would name them; and whatever the man called each living creature, that was its name. So the man gave names to all the livestock, the birds in the sky and all the wild animals. But for Adam no suitable helper was found. So the LORD God caused the man to fall into a deep sleep; and while he was sleeping, he took one of the man's ribs and then closed up the place with flesh. Then the LORD God made a woman from the rib he had taken out of man, and he brought her to the man. The man said, "This is now bone of my bones and flesh of my flesh; she shall be called 'woman,' for she was taken out of man."*

She was made because Adam could not find any of the animals that were comparable or like him. But soon after GOD made Eve from Adam's rib he quickly realized that he had found his companion or help meet. It is important to remember that GOD decided to MAKE ADAM (the man) a help meet. But Adam knew the one for him when GOD presented her. Could there be single men today who are not recognizing their help meet that GOD presents to them? Is this because they are not sensitive to GOD or living in "the Garden of Eden," which is that place of intimacy with GOD? And perhaps women are not yet made by GOD because of not totally submitting to the Lord and his will for their lives.

When you totally submit yourself to the Lord, he helps you as a single Christian to grow spiritually, mentally, socially, intellectually, and financially. God has a specific plan for your life. He makes you wait for various reasons and sometimes you delay marriage yourselves by not submitting to the Lord. Am I saying that everyone that is now married has totally submitted everything to the Lord? Of course not, but this is a point worth digesting if you find yourself still single. Wouldn't you say it is best to have totally submitted to the Lord before marriage, rather than have to learn how to submit to him during marriage? Selah!

Chapter 10
Steps to Spiritual Growth

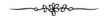

What to Do While You Wait

What are you supposed to do while you wait on God to bring your mate? I believe you can find the answer in Psalms 37:1-8. *Do not fret because of those who are evil or be envious of those who do wrong; for like the grass they will soon wither, like green plants they will soon die away. Trust in the LORD and do good; dwell in the land and enjoy safe pasture. Take delight in the LORD and he will give you the desires of your heart. Commit your way to the Lord; trust in him and he will do this: He will make your righteous reward shine like the dawn, your vindication like the noonday sun. Be still before the LORD and wait patiently for him; do not fret when people succeed in their ways, when they carry out their wicked schemes. Refrain from anger and turn from wrath; do not fret—it leads only to evil.*

TRUST AND DO GOOD

You either trust God or yourself. If you trust in the Lord and do good, then you will dwell in the land of milk and honey. You will feed on God's faithfulness. Do good to yourself as well as to others. How do you do this? It is done through being other-centered, finding your purpose and fulfilling it, being a giver, cultivating Christian friendships, increasing in knowledge and wisdom, enjoying God's creation, and other creative, but godly enjoyments.

PUT YOUR CONFIDENCE IN GOD

Why do you want to put your confidence in someone who thinks like you (Psalms 118:8, Proverbs 3:5)? Why not put your trust in God who does not even think or act as you do? Listen to what the Lord says. For my thoughts are not your thoughts, neither are your ways my ways, declares the LORD. As the heavens are higher than the earth, so are my ways higher than your ways, and my thoughts than your thoughts *(Isaiah 55:8, 9)*.

TRANSFORM YOUR MIND

When you get your mind transformed by the word of God your thoughts become more agreeable to his thoughts. When this happens you have the mind of Christ, although there will still be some things that you will not be able to comprehend. This difference is what makes God to be the Father and you the son or daughter.

DELIGHT/COMMIT/REST/CEASE
HOW DO YOU DELIGHT?

How do you delight? You delight by obeying God's word. Get a personal relationship with Christ if you are not a Christian. You need to praise and worship the Lord and seek him for your purpose in this world. Enjoy Jesus! You should be happy in your relationship with Jesus. As much as possible you should have regular time alone with Him. Learn to have great pleasure in the Lord. Let your spirit delight itself in the Lord. (Isaiah 58:14, Romans 7:22)

GOD IS IN CHARGE

Put God in charge of your life. When you trust in God, you rely on Him. You are commanded to put action behind God's word (Psalms 55:22). Rest is one of the most challenging things for singles and Christians to do. Rest means to literally sleep. Resting should be a state of mind at all times. You should set aside quiet time with the Lord each day and experience his peace, love and joy. Rest in the Lord.

STOP BRIEFLY

Wait upon him, which simply means to stop briefly. Be expectant and endure without complaint. (Matthew 11:28-30) Stop being angry. Do you want to fight with God because he is not moving fast enough for you? Please do not try to help God because he does not need it. Would you agree? I know. I have tried to fight with him and amazingly I always lose. Instead, you need to ask him to help you. Your anger should turn into joy when you look back over your life. God saved you from unhealthy relationships and unholy living. If you are not yet a Christian I want you to know that you too can live holy.

FINDING YOUR PURPOSE and DESTINY
SET APART FOR GOD

This is what God can use in your life to keep you focused and full of joy. God knew what your purpose was before you were born and even before your parents knew that you were conceived. Therefore, you are not an accident, but you are very important to the Lord. He is the one who has ordained your destiny. *Jeremiah 1.5* says, "Before I formed you in the womb I knew you, before you were born I set you apart; I appointed you as a prophet to the nations."

HANDCRAFTED BY GOD

God created every part of you. This includes your inward self as well as your outward being. He took the time to weave every detail of your features. He made you unique and beautiful. You are so very different that no one else can copy your fingerprints or footprints. God took the time and preciseness to make you different from billions and billions and billions of people. There is only one like you. Now *that* to me is very special. There may be someone who tries to be like you, but they will never truly be you. That is something to rejoice about.

FEARFULLY AND WONDERFULLY MADE
Read what *Psalms 139.13-16* says. "For you created my inmost being; you knit me together in my mother's womb. I praise you because I am fearfully and wonderfully made; your works are wonderful, I know that full well. My frame was not hidden from you when I was made in the secret place. When I was woven together in the depths of the earth, your eyes saw my unformed body. All the days ordained for me were written in your book before one of them came to me."

PAST EXPERIENCE AND PURPOSE
All that the Lord has brought you out of, or helped you with in your life can be a building block for him to use you to help someone else. You will flow in your purpose because of this. All you need to do is be obedient to God's word. Your past experiences play a part in your purpose, even though some of them you may not want to remember. Every trial and test that you have gone through, or may be going through now God uses it for His glory and purpose. Knowing and acting on the word of God helps you to be obedient to the plans that he has personally for you.

WORKING IT OUT FOR A PURPOSE
*Romans 8.28-31*encourages the believer in pursuing his or her purpose. "And you know that in all things God works for the good of those who love him, who have been called according to his purpose.

For those God foreknew he also predestined to be conformed to the image of his Son, that he might be the firstborn among many brothers and sisters. And those he predestined, he also called; those he called, he also justified; those he justified, he also glorified. What, then, shall you say in response to these things? If God is for us, who can be against us?"

THROUGH GOD'S STRENGTH

Do not put your trust in yourself or try to do things in your own strength, but use God's strength. God's strength is Christ, the anointed one, who is also the word of God. God's strength comes through God's word. *Philippians 4.13* says, "I can do all this through him who gives me strength." God can use anything and anyone. If God uses someone that the world rejects God's power can be more evident and the person's witness more credible, because God gets all the glory. This is shown in the word of God that follows. *"Brothers and sisters, think of what you were when you were called. Not many of you were wise by human standards; not many were influential; not many were of noble birth. But God chose the foolish things of the world to shame the wise; God chose the weak things of the world to shame the strong. God chose the lowly things of this world and the despised things- and the things that are not-to nullify the things that are, so that no one may boast before him* (I Corinthians 1.26-29)."

EXCHANGE WEAKNESS FOR GOD'S GRACE

God's grace and power is evident in our weaknesses. You should boast, not about yourself, but about what God can do in your shortcomings. Then, you can change your weaknesses for Christ's strength. *2 Corinthians 12.9-10* lets us see this. "But he said to me, 'My grace is sufficient for you, for my power is made perfect in weakness.' Therefore I will boast all the more gladly about my weaknesses, so that Christ's power may rest on me. That is why, for

Christ's sake, I delight in weaknesses, in insults, in hardships, in persecutions, in difficulties. For when I am weak, then I am strong." Because you have Christ's strength, which is the Holy Spirit in you and the word of God, you are able to achieve your goals and visions that the Lord has given you. If you do not have personal goals, you may be in a position to yield to temptation more easily. Being an idle person is not God's plan for anyone. God has a personal vision or plan for each one of us.

HELPFUL TIPS

Here are some pointers that might prove helpful. I want to first of all say that this list is not all-inclusive. These are things that I personally believe will help you find peace, joy, and purpose in the LORD. Remember, I have been single all my life and learning through mistakes is the most difficult and painful road to take, but can be the most life changing and lasting.

ACCEPT CHRIST JESUS AS SAVIOR AND MAKE HIM LORD

Romans 10.8-10-Amplified Bible
"But what does it say? The Word (God's message in Christ) is near you, on your lips and in your heart; that is, the Word (the message, the basis, the object) of faith which you preach, Because if you acknowledge and confess with your lips that Jesus is LORD and in your heart believe (adheres to, trusts in, and relies on the truth) that God raised him from the dead, you will be saved. For with the heart a person believes (adheres to, trusts in, and relies on Christ) and so is justified (declared righteous, acceptable to God), and with the mouth he confesses (declares openly and speaks out freely his faith) and confirms [his] salvation.

John 3.16-18-Amplified Bible

For God so greatly loved and dearly prized the world that He [even] gave up His only begotten (unique) Son, so that whoever believes in (trusts in, clings to, relies on) Him shall not perish (come to destruction, be lost) but have eternal (everlasting) life. For God did not send the Son into the world in order to judge (to reject, to condemn, to pass sentence on) the world, but that the world might find salvation and be made safe and sound through Him. He who believes in Him [who clings to, trusts in, relies on Him] is not judged [he who trusts in Him never comes up for judgment; for him there is no rejection, no condemnation---he incurs no damnation]; but he who does not believe (cleave to, rely on, trust in Him) is judged already [he has already been convicted and has already received his sentence] because he has not believed in and trusted in the name of the only begotten Son of God. [He is condemned for refusing to let his trust rest in Christ's name.]

TELL OTHERS ABOUT THE GOSPEL AND SEEK TO GROW AS A CHRISTIAN BY STUDYING THE WORD

II Timothy 2.15-Amplified Bible

Study and be eager to do your utmost to present yourself to God approved (tested by trial), a workman who has no cause to be ashamed, correctly analyzing and accurately dividing [rightly handling and skillfully teaching] the Word of Truth.

Romans 12.1, 2-Amplified Bible

I APPEAL to you therefore, brethren, and beg of you in view of [all] the mercies of God, to make a decisive dedication of your bodies [presenting all your members and faculties] as a living sacrifice, holy (devoted, consecrated) and well pleasing to God, which is your reasonable (rational, intelligent) service and spiritual worship. Do not be conformed to this world (this age), [fashioned after and adapted to its external, superficial customs], but be transformed (changed) by the [entire] renewal of your mind [by its new ideals and its new attitude], so that you may prove [for yourselves] what is the good and acceptable and perfect will of God, even the thing which is good and acceptable and perfect [in His sight for you.]

DO WHATEVER IT TAKES TO NOT HAVE UN-CONFESSED SIN IN YOUR LIFE.

I John 1.9-Amplified Bible
If we [freely] confess that we have sinned and confess our sins, He is faithful and just (true to His own nature and promises) and will forgive our sins [dismiss our lawlessness] and [continuously] cleanse us from all unrighteousness [everything not in conformity to His will in purpose, thought, and action].

Ephesians 4.26-Amplified Bible
When angry, do not sin; do not ever let your wrath (your exasperation, your fury or indignation) last until the sun goes down.

PRAY AND COMMUNE WITH GOD THROUGH THE HOLY SPIRIT DAILY AND BE A DOER OF HIS WORD

Ephesians 6.18-Amplified Bible
Pray at all times (on every occasion, in every season) in the Spirit, with all [manner of] prayer and entreaty. To that end keep alert watch with strong purpose and perseverance, interceding in behalf of all the saints (God's consecrated people).

James 1.22-Amplified Bible
But be doers of the word [obey the message], and not merely listeners to it, betraying yourselves [into deception by reasoning contrary to the Truth].

LISTEN WHEN PRAYING, MEDITATING AND STUDYING SPECIFICALLY FOR DIRECTION THROUGH THE HOLY SPIRIT AND THROUGH GOD'S WORD

John 10.4,5-Amplified Bible
When he has brought his own sheep outside, he walks on before them, and the sheep follow him because they know his voice. They will never [on any account] follow a stranger, but will run away from him because they do not know the voice of strangers or recognize their call.

James 1.1-Amplified Bible
Understand [this], my beloved brethren. Let every man be quick to hear [a ready listener], slow to speak, slow to take offense and to get angry.

FIND GOD'S SPIRITUAL GIFT(S) AND YOUR SPECIFIC PURPOSE ON EARTH IN HIS TIMING.

Ecclesiastes 3.1-Amplified Bible
To everything there is a season, and a time for every matter or purpose under heaven.

I Corinthians 12.8-11-Amplified Bible
To one is given in and through the [Holy] Spirit [the power to speak] a message of wisdom, and to another [the power to express] a word of knowledge and understanding according to the same [Holy]

Spirit; To another [wonder working] faith by the same [Holy] Spirit, to another the extraordinary powers of healing by the one Spirit; To another the working of miracles, to another prophetic insight (the gift of interpreting the divine will and purpose); to another the ability to discern and distinguish between [the utterances of true] spirits [and false ones], to another various kinds of [unknown] tongues, to another the ability to interpret [such] tongues. All these [gifts, achievements, abilities] are inspired and brought to pass by one and the same [Holy] Spirit, Who apportions to each person individually [exactly] as He chooses.

BE EFFECTIVE, NOT JUST BUSY

Be effective, not just busy. Continue to do things that you enjoy and have patience while waiting on the possibility of marriage. Set realistic, but challenging goals for your life based upon your desires and the purpose of God or even what you might think your purpose is. You will not always know everything perfectly, but it will be revealed over time and through life experiences. I have found that you need to get started doing something and as you travel the road searching you will be directed and redirected to the path that God has for you. Always continue to grow spiritually, mentally, emotionally, socially, intellectually, and financially. Above all else, make God your first love.

QUESTIONS ABOUT PURPOSE

Following is a list of questions that will help you begin to know the direction of your specific purpose. Of course, you will need to be prayerful about it as well, but don't become stressful about it. *RELAX.* Ask yourself these questions and please answer them truthfully to the best of your ability. If you do not honestly know the answer then that is okay. Continue to pray, study the word, and ask God through the Holy Spirit. Be prepared to be patient and wait on the answer. He may give you an immediate answer or it may be days, weeks, months or even years before he reveals to you his complete plan. Your purpose will usually be revealed step by step. As you complete each step you will find another piece to the puzzle. But listen as he reveals to you step-by-step and obey each step because it is a test of your obedience as well. Also, listen as others tell you what you are good at and what they sense God has put into you.

ASK YOURSELF

What do you I like doing?

What things am I good at and what do others compliment me on?

What excites me? What am I passionate about?

What comes easy to me?

Do I like working with things or people?

What am I doing now? Why am I doing it? Do I like it? Why or why not?

What have I done in the past and what did I like or dislike about it?

If I could do anything I wanted to do and there are not any obstacles what would I do?

What am I doing now that may be helping or hindering my desires or purpose?

What do I think my purpose might be? Why do I think this?

PRAYER OF SALVATION: If you are not a born-again believer

Dear Lord Jesus, come into my heart right now. Lord, I confess that I have sinned. But you say if I admit my sins, have a change of heart, you will forgive my sins and make me clean, make me whole. I believe that.

Thank you Lord Jesus for cleansing me and for saving me. Amen!

PRAYER OF REDICATION: If you are a believer, but are out of fellowship with the Lord

Dear Lord Jesus, forgive me for turning my back on you and for not been faithful. I confess that I have sinned. But you say that if I confess my sins, you would forgive me. I believe that.

Thank you Lord Jesus for forgiving me, making me whole and giving me another chance. Amen!

PRAYER FOR BAPTISM WITH THE HOLY SPIRIT-You need more power and strength

Dear Lord Jesus, I am a Christian. Thank you for saving me. Lord, I want to experience the baptism with the Holy Spirit. The Holy Spirit came into my heart when I became a Christian, but I want to experience more power. You say in your word that every good and perfect gift comes from above and that you give it freely. So baptize me now with the free gift of the Holy Spirit. I receive it now. I will open my mouth and let the tongues flow out by faith.

In Jesus name. Amen!

A Word Of Thanks

I want to thank you for purchasing and reading my very first of many books that I believe that I am purposed to write. My number one goal for writing is for ministry. I want to help you as a reader to realize that God cares about you so very much. As a Christian leader who has been through quite a few challenges in life I want to see you experience the love, joy and peace of God. I have been on the other side and now I am on the side of love, joy and peace and I asked myself, "Why did you wait so long?" Well, I didn't know what I was missing. The difference was between religion, relationship and fellowship. This is often how the life of Christians progress. But that is not God's plan. He wants you to be a part of the Kingdom of God and not religion. He wants you to have a personal (talking, fellowshipping, loving) relationship with Jesus Christ. Many people are not joyful and content because they are experiencing religion and not the fellowship of God. You will know that you have moved from religion to fellowship when you realize that God counts you, yes you, as HIS friend. I can say without a doubt today that "I am a friend of God (Jesus and the Holy Spirit)."

I want to leave you with a very popular, often quoted, but in my opinion, not a very often believed scripture from Jeremiah 29.11 from *The Message Bible.*

I know what I am doing. I have it all planned out-plans to take care of you, not abandon you, plans to give you the future you hoped for.

YOU ARE

You are always on my mind
Sweetheart
You are always on my mind
Sweetheart
You're the apple of my eye
So don't be surprised
Of all the things
I do for you
You are always on my heart
Daughter (Son)
You are always on my heart
Daughter (Son)
There's not a day that goes by
When I'm not thinking of you
You have a special place
In me, you do

January 26, 2001
d. Yvonne Shotwell

Father God, In Jesus name, I pray that you show your faithfulness toward this one here Lord. Don't forget your promises concerning them. You are a faithful God and you know everything you have planned. Give them daily assurance that you hold them in the palm of your hand and each day you are bringing together another piece of the puzzle for their purpose and destiny. *IN JESUS NAME!*

You may visit the following website for more reading materials, updates on my writing and ministry. It would encourage me if you sent me a short word of encouragement about how the book blessed you and any prayer requests that you may have.

Thank you for investing in your future.

Contact Information: www.daisyshotwellministries.com

About the Author

d. Yvonne Shotwell, a graduate of Oral Roberts University, is a prophet, business woman, educator, and author. She was released into prophetic office through Apostolic Movement International in San Diego, California. She is the founder of Daisy Shotwell Ministries in and owner of Daisy Communications, LLC. Prophet "Yvonne" has been in ministry for 22 years and has served internationally as a missionary pastor and teacher. She has earned a BBA, MA, and MDiv.